Pass-Along Papers

by
Barbara Kuczen, Ph.D.
and
Carly Kuczen, M.A.

Marietta, Georgia

Copyright ©1999 by Barbara Kuzcen. All rights reserved. The use and copying of this material is subject to a license agreement. Any other use is prohibited. No part of this publication may be transmitted, transcribed, stored in a retrieval system, or translated into any language in any form by any means without the prior written consent of Active Parenting Publishers. Permitted use is limited to one owner of the Pass-Along Papers and may not be transferred to another party. Pass-Along Papers may be duplicated by the owner of the Pass-Along Papers on an unlimited use basis. However, all Pass-Along Papers duplicated must include the Barbara Kuzcen copyright. Use of your set of the Pass-Along Papers indicates your acceptance of these terms. If you do not agree with these terms and conditions, either destroy or return the intact set of Pass-Along Papers to Active Parenting Publishers. This license is in effect from your date of purchase and shall remain in force until terminated. You may terminate the license and this agreement any time by destroying your set of Pass-Along Papers, together with all copies of individual papers in your possession.

Introduction

Parenting.....one of life's most difficult, yet most important jobs. Every parent at times feels stressed, confused, worried, and overwhelmed. The *Pass-Along-Papers* have been designed to provide parents and other adults with useful information to help them understand and deal with the everyday problems of normal children. We have attempted to provide a comprehensive set of thoroughly researched *Papers*, written in nontechnical language. We wanted to enable parent educators, teachers, psychologists, therapists, pediatricians, social workers, and counselors to *Pass-Along* practical, common sense strategies for dealing with the behavior problems that our discussions with educators and parents indicated were most often encountered. We hope that the reference format makes it easy for you to locate and use the information you need.

You will notice that for some concerns there are many possible solutions. We have found that there is no ONE best way to solve any particular problem. It is our hope that you will work closely with the parents to formulate a *Family Action Plan*, based on the complex, individual characteristics and needs of the child within the unique family system. We envision you sitting down with parents and saying, "Here are twenty-eight ways to build self-esteem. What do you think will work best for you and your child?" Please add your own suggestions or the parent's ideas to the *Other Comments and Suggestions* section.

The *Pass-Along-Papers* focus on typical, normal childhood problems. Although these concerns are considered normal, they should not be viewed as unimportant and be left to go away on their own. In some cases you may wonder about the difference between normal and abnormal behavior. There are several criteria to help you decide. First, you must consider intensity, as well as how often the behavior causes a problem for the child, parent, or others. If it frequently causes disruption, professional counseling, therapy, or treatment might be indicated. Second, if a child has a number of different problems, this fact may also signal a need for professional intervention. Third, the more age inappropriate the behavior, the more serious the problem. Finally, if the problem has persisted for a long time and seems to resist the positive steps to correct it, more aggressive treatment may be required. Remind parents of the necessity for communicating clearly defined expectations and rules. Also, the techniques suggested in the *Pass-Along-Papers* won't work unless carried out with faithful consistency.

Contents

Introduction

Topic:	Pass-Along-Paper
Aggressive behavior	*1*
Anxiety	*2*
Attention-span	*3*
Bad manners	*4*
Bedtime problems	*5*
Bed-wetting	*6*
Blaming others	*7*
Crisis coping	*8*
Crying	*9*
Cursing	*10*
Death	*11*
Defiant behavior	*12*
Discipline	*13*
Divorce	*14*
Eating (overeating)	*15*
Eating (poor)	*16*
Education	*17*
Fears	*18*
Friends	*19*
Gifted child	*20*
Hyperactivity	*21*
Impulsiveness	*22*
Inappropriate behavior	*23*
Independence	*24*

Jealousy	*25*
Learning disabilities	*26*
Lying	*27*
Medical visits	*28*
Negativism	*29*
Overindulgence	*30*
Poor loser	*31*
Problem-solving	*32*
Responsibility	*33*
Risk-taking	*34*
Self-esteem	*35*
Sexual behavior	*36*
Shyness	*37*
Sibling rivalry	*38*
Speech problems	*39*
Stealing	*40*
Step-families	*41*
Stress-breakers	*42*
Stress-coping	*43*
Stress-signals	*44*
Talking back	*45*
Tantrums	*46*
Tattling	*47*
Teasing	*48*
Television	*49*
Time-quality	*50*
Violence	*51*
Whining	*52*

NOTICE TO THE READER

The ideas, procedures, and suggestions contained in the *Pass-Along-Papers* are not intended as a substitute for consulting with medical or mental health professionals. Problems of a serious nature should involve a referral to an appropriate professional in your community.

Workshops and Lectures

If you are interested in learning about our workshops and lectures, please contact us at:

Children's Stress Institute
121 Timber View Drive
Oak Brook, Illinois 60523
Telephone: (630) 530-5511
Fax: (630)-530-2929

Aggressive or Hostile Behavior   Pass-Along-Paper 1

✏️ *<u>Description of the problem:</u>* Aggression and hostility are the fight response in the fight-or-flight reaction to stress. Hostility is characterized by unfriendliness or opposition and can ultimately lead to aggression, whereby a child attempts to do damage to a person or thing. The assault may be physical or verbal. A child's rude behavior, sarcasm, or silence can be exasperating or even frightening to a parent. There's an urge to set the child straight with a slap, shaking, or command to "snap out of it!" Actually, confrontation is the worst possible alternative. Generally, children want either to be left alone or to be allowed to blow up. In both cases it is important that the child realize that someone understands, but children struggling to assert their independence may initially reject parents' offers to help. If your child does not accept the invitation to talk it out, try to stay out of the way until the emotional storm has subsided. However, rude or violent behavior affects the entire family and cannot be tolerated simply because the child is in a bad mood. In this case the child must be firmly told: "I can see you are troubled. I'd like to help. If you want to be left alone until you feel better, that's okay, too. However, your behavior is upsetting everyone. I don't want to make your problems worse by becoming angry, so please control yourself."

✏️ *<u>Factors influencing the problem:</u>* Although most behavior is learned, understanding the temperamental differences among children can help to explain why some children are more prone to aggression than others. In addition, some adults directly sanction aggressive behavior when they advise children to "stand up for themselves and don't take anything from anybody." Also, when we allow aggression to prove a satisfying method for dealing with stress, the child is inclined to continue its use. For example, if Amy experiences satisfaction at her power to strike a playmate and make her cry, Amy is apt to continue hitting. If Jack learns that when he grabs a toy from his older brother, his parents will probably say: "Oh, let Jack have it! He's younger than you," Jack will frequently rely on this technique.

In some cases children engage in aggressive acts because they crave attention so much that they will settle for any kind they can get—even if it is negative. Obviously, these children need more attention for desirable behavior and minimal attention for the undesirable. When the child behaves aggressively, tell the child to go to his or her room until the child feels better and can behave properly. In this way your disapproval is communicated without providing undue attention, which reinforces this pattern of behavior.

Children find models for aggressive behavior wherever they turn. Not only is violence found in entertainment and news accounts, it is also demonstrated by the peer group, teachers, and parents. As one puzzled parent put it: "I can't understand why Jamie keeps hitting her sister. She must have gotten spanked a hundred times for doing that." Physical punishment provides a model for the aggressive behavior you are telling the child is unacceptable. In effect, you are telling the child, "Do as I say, not as I do."

Frustration is the disappointment or defeat experienced by a child who doesn't get what he or she wants, which can range from a plaything to the love and attention of a parent. Adults should avoid making conflicting, developmentally inappropriate, or petty demands that are difficult—if not impossible—to meet. Frustration can also be reduced by moving into some situations before they get out of hand. For example, wild, rough-and-tumble play almost always results in accidental, minor injury which can prompt an aggressive reaction in the victim. Allow children to work through their own problems, but when you see they've reached the point where they simply can't cope, help settle the matter before a fight erupts. In other words, frustration can be minimized by establishing an environment that is not over directed, and yet not under directed. Over permissiveness is just as frustrating as over-control to the child who wants and needs limits that show love and concern. In addition, we must guard against paradox parenting, in which we approve of or ignore an act of aggression one day, only to jump all over the child for the same behavior at a future time.

✎ *Suggestions:*

1. Observe the aggressive behavior and try to determine the situational triggers.
2. Communicate to the child clearly and specifically which behaviors are not allowed and what the consequences of such behaviors will be. Let the child know that aggressive feelings are a natural response to stress, and that control doesn't mean suppressing them, but instead learning more acceptable means to express anger.
3. React to specific instances of aggressive behavior quickly and firmly; consequences should be a logical outcome of the behavior and follow immediately. Punishment should take the form previously specified to the child and should be consistently applied.
4. The punishment should <u>not</u> be physical (or even verbally aggressive), as this simply validates and reinforces aggressive behavior as a means for solving problems.
5. While it is important to be firm, don't be confrontational. Calmly discuss the problem with the child, try to understand why the child behaved aggressively, and guide the child toward alternative ways to deal with problems.
6. Ignore attention-getting ploys. If the aggressive behavior seems to be an attempt to attract attention, don't let it work. Let the behavior run its course (unless, of course, it threatens the safety of the child or others), and then enforce consequences quickly and <u>briefly</u>. "Time-outs" can be effective along these lines.
7. Encourage activities (e.g. physical, creative) that allow the child to vent anger and aggression harmlessly and in socially appropriate ways.
8. Use positive reinforcement when the child makes progress and avoids the temptation to behave aggressively in a difficult situation. Remember, if your child is highly aggressive, the child might have learned that aggression is the most effective way to gain attention or to solve problems.
9. Provide a positive example by controlling your own aggression - thus showing the child how to cope with people and problems in a more constructive manner.
10. Limit the child's exposure to violence on television and in the media.
11. Following an act of aggression, discuss the matter with your child. Tell the child you understand his or her feelings with remarks such as, "I know how important it was to you to get a turn on the swing." Encourage the child to generate alternative, satisfying approaches to aggression. Talk about how the child might respond the next time, perhaps even role-playing the situation.
12. Foster a general appreciation of the consequences of one's actions on other people and encourage a sense of concern for others.
13. Address the possible root causes of aggressive behavior, such as lack of confidence, frustration, high stress, or lack of affection. In general, a happier, less stressed child who receives affection and encouragement and who learns how to deal with frustration will be less likely to behave aggressively.
14. Provide your child with opportunities for independence and decision-making so he or she does not feel smothered by authority and compelled to rebel.

<u>OTHER COMMENTS OR SUGGESTIONS</u>:

FAMILY ACTION PLAN: (List suggestion numbers of particular relevance and specific actions planned)

Copyright ©1999 by Barbara Kuczen. Published by

Anxiety
Pass-Along-Paper 2

✎ *Description of the problem:* On the surface, anxiety looks a lot like fear. The anxious child appears agitated and may cry or scream easily. The child may have difficulty sleeping, have frequent nightmares, eat poorly, or have obsessive thoughts. Anxiety can lead to sweating, butterflies in the stomach, nausea, breathing difficulties, or tics. However, it is much easier to deal with fear than with anxiety. The major difference being that fear has a specific, known cause, while anxiety is reflected in a nonspecific sense of uneasiness. When dealing with fear, the parent need only to remove or control the threat, and fear vanishes. Anxiety is another matter. It causes the child's thought processes to become disorganized and reduces concentration. Anxiety can have a spiral effect. Once the child begins to worry, the worry seems to feed on itself. One troublesome thought leads to another, and the child becomes convinced that he or she can't cope, saying or thinking things like, "Why does this always happen to me?"

✎ *Factors influencing the problem:* Now and then, stressful events in a child's life can lead to perfectly normal anxiety. Problems develop when the child's anxiety has grown out of proportion to life's realistic stresses. Anxious children are often "worry warts" and are easily frightened. They can be inordinately cautious, rigid, inflexible, and indecisive. Frequently they seem ill at ease or apprehensive and have lowered self-esteem. Anxious children can become excessively dependent on adults. Anxiety can be the result of many factors. It is important to help your child identify what is "bugging" him or her. Once the child becomes aware of overreacting, the child can pull the reigns on runaway worrying and regain control. See if any of the problems listed below might be your child's cause of anxiety:

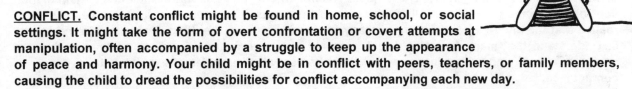

CONFLICT. Constant conflict might be found in home, school, or social settings. It might take the form of overt confrontation or covert attempts at manipulation, often accompanied by a struggle to keep up the appearance of peace and harmony. Your child might be in conflict with peers, teachers, or family members, causing the child to dread the possibilities for conflict accompanying each new day.

PRESSURE. The highly competitive nature of our society influences children at an early age. Some very young children have developed the habit of near-compulsive overdoing. They are over-programmed or just keep push-push-pushing. Relief never seems to be in sight, since two new activities take the place of each one completed. Overly critical adults may make the child feel compelled to achieve perfection.

INCONSISTENCY. Children today receive conflicting, confusing role messages. In many ways they are urged to hurry and grow up, and they develop a maturity far in advance of that possessed by their parents at the same age. The entrance of large numbers of mothers into the work force has made it necessary for some children to fend for themselves. In addition, adults may make life unpredictable and scary by inconsistently communicating expectations and enforcing rules.

BURNOUT. Few adults think about burnout in terms of children. Executives, air traffic controllers, or teachers burn out—not youngsters. The overprogrammed life led by many children can lead to burnout. Children who spend hours away from home each day in day care or move from one activity to another in a state of chronic, uncontrolled stress can suffer from feelings of exhaustion and depression.

LONELINESS. Children can be lonely not only when they are alone but when they are integrally involved with family, class mates, or friends. Loneliness stems from a sense of isolation or a feeling that no one really cares about you. It can also arise from rejection, especially if the child is overly dependent on one person in particular, or on others in general. Many children of busy parents experience profound loneliness and rejection.

INFERIORITY. Feelings of inferiority result from the agony of real or imagined human limitations or disadvantages. The individual may feel inferior to others in terms of background, appearance, intelligence, coping ability, or success.

LIFE CHANGE. Major life changes occur with regularity. Births, deaths, divorce, a parent's new job, moving, or serious illness are but a few examples of upheavals that require major life adjustments. Until the adjustment is made, the child functions in a state of general uneasiness.

SELF-IMAGE. The protection of one's own self-image is a natural, healthy drive. Some children become anxious because parents, peers, teachers, or they themselves have set standards and expectations that are unrealistic and unattainable. The goal is to "go out there and knock 'em dead" each and every day. After a few failures, children may lose confidence and feel tense about life in general.

Suggestions:

1. Work on any of the issues identified above.
2. Anxious parents usually have anxious children. They create an air of constant tension. Don't overprotect your child. Model optimism, coupled with healthy cautiousness.
3. Realize that a child is bound to worry more once the child realizes that adults cannot guarantee safety and hence loses his or her immature, magical view of the world.
4. Avoid instilling fear in children and instead model good problem solving. When children worry, help them figure out options and different courses of action to prevent a difficult situation or to cope with an existing problem.
5. Recognize that many of your child's questions reflect underlying worries. Don't laugh at them or dismiss them with a hasty reply. These questions are an effort on the part of the child to gain mental control of feelings or worries. Although some of their questions seem to reflect needless worries, realize that the child may be plotting strategy for how to deal with a difficult situation in the future.
6. Understand that many fantasies about personal glory are a normal way to achieve feelings of mastery. Identifying with dinosaurs or super-heroes also provides the child with a sense of competence.
7. Don't criticize or tease the child for foolishly worrying. Instead, provide a safe, reassuring atmosphere. Rather than trying to discourage the child from worrying, help the child logically analyze the worry and put it into realistic perspective.
8. Help the child build feelings of independence (*Pass-Along-Paper 24*) and self-esteem (*Pass-Along-Paper 35*).

OTHER COMMENTS OR SUGGESTIONS:

FAMILY ACTION PLAN: (List suggestion numbers of particular relevance and specific actions planned)

Attention Span

Pass-Along-Paper 3

Description of the problem: The child stays with activities for a shorter period of time than other children of the same age or developmental level. When the child is interrupted, the child frequently does not go back to the same activity. When the child is learning something new, the child is easily frustrated and wants to do something else. If you are too busy to answer a question, the child might go away and not come back later for the answer. The child with a short attention span dislikes doing the same thing for a long period of time and doesn't finish what is started. If the child has difficulty with something, the child looks for immediate assistance, rather than trying to figure it out. The child with short attention span may have difficulty sitting still, organizing work or play activities, finishing projects, or focusing. He or she may be very easily distracted. The ability to focus on a task and stick to it is essential for school success, so children with a short attention span have a problem.

Factors influencing the problem: Attention span is a component of temperament. Short attention span can be associated with attention deficit disorder. Teachers often find the child with short attention span difficult to manage in school. He or she usually does not stay with a task long enough to get the full benefit. The child may also disrupt the other children and demand a larger share of the teacher's time and attention for negative, rather than positive, behavior. Before you decide that your child has a short attention span, consider the child's age and developmental level. Preschool children naturally prefer to move quickly from one activity to another and need a lot of free choice and child initiated activity. As children grow, their attention spans increase. You should also consider the age-appropriateness of the tasks assigned children. A child may not be able to focus for a long period of time because the activity is too difficult or boring (like listening to adults talk). You should also consider whether or not the child may have a food allergy that contributes to crabbiness and hyperactivity. Finally, is the environment overstimulating and distracting. Excessive noise, movement nearby, heat, or overcrowding may be the cause of a child's inability to pay attention for long.

Suggestions:
1. Begin by providing your child with simple, one-step directions.
2. Reduce or minimize distractions, such as television or visitors.
3. Set up a quiet place for your child to complete tasks.
4. Don't make unreasonable demands - consider your child's age. The more interesting an activity, the longer the child will stay with it. According to experts, the average attention span for a play activity for a two-year-old is seven minutes, for a three-year-old is nine-minutes, for a four-year-old is twelve minutes, and for a five-year-old is fourteen minutes. However, if an activity is particularly demanding, like listening to an adult explain something, children can usually concentrate for about one minute per year old.
5. If you suspect your child has an unusually short attention span for his or her age, discuss your concerns with the child's teachers and doctor.
6. Provide your child with reminders when it is time to complete a task or a chore.
7. Help your child complete a task by breaking it down into smaller, more manageable tasks.
8. Don't give your child responsibilities which are too complicated and involved. Make them simple and easy to complete.
9. Provide your child with supervision, assistance, and gentle reminders while the child is completing a task so that the child won't get sidetracked. Gradually decrease your involvement so that your child works more independently.

10. Before the child starts a task, be certain that all the necessary materials are at hand.
11. Help the child make a list of what must be accomplished and the order in which steps must be done. Some children with attention span problems have difficulty correctly sequencing activities.
12. Set a daily schedule or routine and adhere to it. Post it on the refrigerator and specify the order in which events will take place. Specify the times for getting up, doing homework, taking care of pets, and doing chores.
13. When a child thinks of something that needs to be done, like bringing a field trip permission slip back to school, encourage the child to get it signed and place it in the book bag on the spot, rather than delaying action.
14. If your child has difficulty staying on track while doing homework, sit with the child and read, pay bills, do handicrafts, etc.
15. Work one-to-one with your child on homework or reading, gradually increasing the amount of time the child can focus on an activity. Over the long-term you will want to begin to decrease your involvement so that the child works independently.
16. Play educational games which are fun and build concentration.
17. If your child does not believe that he or she can succeed at a task the child will have little interest in the activity. The child moves from one endeavor to the next to avoid failure. Therefore you should give your child simple, short projects to complete and steer your child away from frustrating games or projects. Encourage and praise your child for succeeding and reinforce feelings of competence.
18. Encourage your child to ask for help instead of giving up.
19. Make certain that your child maintains eye contact with you when you give a set of directions. Keep the directions short and simple. Have your child repeat them back to you.
20. Pay attention to your child when your child is paying attention. Give your child praise and rewards for staying on task. Don't reinforce short attention span by giving the child more attention for not paying attention than for paying attention. If your child won't pay attention, ignore the child until he or she goes back to the activity.
21. Insist that your child clean-up and put away all materials before moving to a new activity.

OTHER COMMENTS OR SUGGESTIONS:

FAMILY ACTION PLAN: (List suggestion numbers of particular relevance and specific actions planned)

Copyright ©1999 by Barbara Kuczen. Published by Active Parenting Publishers
www.activeparenting.com

Bad Manners

Pass-Along-Paper 4

✏️ *Description of the problem:* Manners are largely determined by culture, and bad manners offend many people. The child who burps, pick his or her nose, chews with the mouth open, or doesn't use correct social conventions - like saying please and thank you - seems to be ignorant of society's most basic rules. Bad manners can make your child appear less intelligent.

✏️ *Factors influencing the problem:* Parents have a responsibility to teach their children acceptable manners and social conventions. Parents must realize that good manners are not something you take on and off, like a party outfit, depending on the social situation. Manners are habit, a consistent part of each day. Of course, your child's age will determine what are reasonable expectations.

✏️ *Suggestions:*

1. Model the manners you expect your child to follow both at home and in public.
2. Remind older siblings of their responsibility to model good manners to younger children in the family.
3. At various stages of development, children react hysterically to burps or farts and tend to egg each other on. While this behavior is normal, it is nonetheless bothersome, and you should indicate your disapproval. Don't laugh along with the children one day and become irritated the next.
4. Discuss the obvious reasons for manners such as chewing with your mouth closed, using a tissue, waiting your turn in line, respecting the rights of others, talking quietly in public, or waiting patiently for your turn to speak.
5. Compliment your child when good manners are evident. For example you might say, "I liked the way you held the door open for Grandpa!" or "Your table manners were excellent tonight at dinner."
6. When you child exhibits bad manners, quietly and privately point out what the child did wrong. For example you might say, "Today when Billy was telling us about what happened in gym class you interrupted him twice."
7. Ask the child to tell you how she or he thinks the offended person or persons might have felt. For example, "How do you think Billy felt when you interrupted him? How do you think those who were listening to his story felt?" In the case of a child who chews with his or her mouth open you might express your opinion, "I can't enjoy my meal when I see someone chewing their food with their mouth open."
8. Before an unusual social situation, like a plane trip, funeral or wedding, anticipate potential problems such as talking loudly in public and remind the child of the manners expected.
9. Be consistent in your expectations about manners. Don't laugh when the child burps one time and frown the next.
10. Don't contribute to your child's bad manners. For example, a messy snack at the wrong time or a noisy toy in the wrong place invites trouble.
11. Establish a *secret signal* with which you can easily remind the child of a manners slip. For example, tapping your head to indicate it's time to think about what you are doing or drawing an imaginary line to symbolize a boundary over which the child has stepped.
12. Make it clear that bad manners embarrass the child, the parents, and the observers.
13. If your child is demonstrating bad manners, quietly remove the child from the situation. Clearly point out the inappropriate behavior and do not rejoin the social setting until the child tells you she or he can act in an acceptable fashion.

14. **Don't encourage the child to act silly or cute in front of others and then expect the child to know when enough is enough and it's time to stop or when it's bad timing to act silly.**
15. **Communicate your expectations for your child's manners to relatives, teachers, baby-sitters, and friends.**
16. **Don't act shocked or disgusted when the child demonstrates bad manners. Make it clear it is one small act you disapprove of - not the child. On the contrary, it is because you hold the child in such high regard that you expect high standards.**

OTHER COMMENTS OR SUGGESTIONS:

FAMILY ACTION PLAN: (List suggestion numbers of particular relevance and specific actions planned.)

copyright Children's Stress Institute

Copyright ©1999 by Barbara Kuczen. Published by ACTIVE PARENTING PUBLISHERS
www.activeparenting.com

Bedtime problems　　　　　　　　　　　　　　　　Pass-Along-Paper 5

✏️ *Description of the problem:* Most children go through a phase when they hate going to bed. Young children between the ages of one- to two-and one-half- years old, in particular, resist going to bed and will sometimes awaken during the night and demand attention. The problem may recur at ages four- to six-years-old. Children use many of the *one more* stalling techniques - such as asking for one more drink of water, going to the bathroom one more time, begging for one more story, or demanding one more kiss.

✏️ *Factors influencing the problem:* If the child senses that there is excitement going on after she or he goes to bed, obviously the youngster doesn't want to miss the fun. It is normal and healthy for a child to want to cram as much into each day as possible. Sometimes the child resists bedtime because she or he is simply not tired. Like adults, different children require differing amounts of sleep. A nap may have been taken too late in the day, or the child may just not be tired. Some parents have found that eliminating naptime or moving bedtime back a bit solves the problem. In other cases, a child may fear the dark. As children get older, they may have difficulty sleeping due to noise, worries, or overstimulation.

✏️ *Suggestions:*
1. Set fixed wake-up and bedtimes for school days and for week-ends. Establish routines for bathing, quiet time, prayers, snacks, or story time. Follow the routine consistently so that your child will settle into a regular sleep/awake cycle.
2. Make the time before bed as relaxing as possible. Avoid overstimulation by turning off the television and discouraging highly active or rough play. Don't watch frightening or upsetting movies or television programs right before bedtime.
3. A warm bath and snack can make the child more ready for sleep, but avoid beverages with caffeine such as colas or iced tea.
4. Give your child advanced warning that it is time to prepare for bed.
5. Make bedtime a special, warm, pleasant time that the child enjoys. Set aside fifteen minutes for a massage, story, or chat.
6. Children love rituals, and bedtime rituals make them feel safe and secure. Your child might kiss everyone and then say a prayer or sing a song.
7. Don't allow your child to start watching a program which will continue past bedtime. If you do let the child start viewing a program plan to videotape the ending for viewing the next day.
8. Don't punish your child by sending him or her to bed, which can cause the child to view bedtime as negative.
9. Encourage everyone to prepare for bed at the same time so that the younger child doesn't think everyone else is up having fun.
10. Once the child has gone to bed and you leave the room, tell the child you are not coming back. Ignore the child's cries or whining, and they will usually disappear in a few minutes. If the child is ill, wet, injured, or frightened comfort the child. However, if the child is just crying for attention, providing that attention only reinforces the behavior. Visit the child's room every twenty minutes to wipe the tears, and leave immediately.
11. If the child complains of not being tired, tell the child to just rest quietly in bed until he or she falls asleep.
12. Allow the child to take a security object or blanket to bed.
13. If you sense that your child is truly not sleepy, consider eliminating naps or moving bed time back.

14. Be certain that there are no loud distractions close to your child's bedroom. If they can't be avoided, consider playing some quiet classical music or a tape of ocean or forest sounds.

15. Don't make fun of the child for being afraid of the dark. Instead, listen sympathetically and help the child check the closet and under the bed. Get a nightlight and rearrange furniture to get rid of troublesome shadows. Allow the child to keep a flashlight under his or her pillow. Let a sibling or a pet sleep in the room with the child. Above all, don't ever threaten a child with the *bogeyman,* avoid frightening movies and television programs, and stay away from the more violent fairy tales.

16. Some parents lie down for a few minutes with their child. However, it is better not to allow the child to develop the habit of getting into bed with the parents.

17. Overstimulation or stress can lead to bad dreams or nightmares. Children as young as eighteen months have been reported with bad dreams. Between the ages of one and four bad dreams occur occasionally. Nightmares commonly become a problem between four and six years old, although in one study twenty-eight percent of the children between the ages of six- and twelve-years-old still had them. A nightmare is more frightening than a bad dream. It causes a child to awake in terror. The parent should turn on the light and cuddle the child until he or she is fully awake. Comfort the child with reassurance that it was only a bad dream and that you are close by. The child may prefer to have a light left on or the door left open. You should stay with the child until he or she is ready to fall back to sleep, but it is better not to take the child into bed with you.

OTHER COMMENTS OR SUGGESTIONS:

FAMILY ACTION PLAN: (List suggestion numbers of particular relevance and specific actions planned)

Copyright ©1999 by Barbara Kuczen. Published by ACTIVE PARENTING PUBLISHERS
www.activeparenting.com

Bed-wetting　　　　　　　　　　　　　　　　Pass-Along-Paper 6

Description of the problem: Bed-wetting or nocturnal enuresis is the involuntary elimination of urine during sleep. Approximately five to seven million children wet their beds at night. It is a very common childhood problem affecting 40% of 3-year-olds, 10% of 6-year-olds and 3% of 12-year-olds. Girls tend to gain control of the bladder earlier in life than boys, and most experts would not be concerned about a child who wets the bed at 4 or even 5-years-old. Most doctors will not treat bed-wetting as a problem until at least the age of 6. However, no matter what the child's age, bed-wetting is embarrassing and frustrating for both parents and children. By puberty, most bed-wetters have outgrown enuresis, although research shows that 1% or 2% of 16-year-olds are occasional bed-wetters.

Factors influencing the problem: Although bed-wetting is annoying, most parents are tolerant of the problem in toddlers. However, as the child grows older, parents often become more impatient. Bed-wetting can also impact friendships with peers, as the child becomes apprehensive that friends will learn of the problem. Most bed-wetters shy away from slumber parties and camping trips and may feel left out. They may not like family trips, either, preferring to sleep in their own beds so that relatives or hotel maids won't learn the secret. In severe cases, bed-wetting can even result in lowered self-esteem and poor school performance. Experts have discussed bed-wetting for years, and there is still divided opinion about its cause. Most agree that bladder size and family history of bed-wetting are factors. Recent research indicates that some bed-wetters may have less of an antidiuretic hormone which limits the production of urine output at night. As a result, these children make four times the normal amount of nighttime urine and are more likely to exceed their bladder's capacity. No matter what the cause, children should be directly involved in managing their own bed-wetting problem. It gives them a positive feeling of taking action and a sense of personal control.

Suggestions:

1. Remember that occasional accidents are a normal part of growing up. Most bed-wetting disappears on its own over time.
2. Don't become angry with your bed-wetting child. Remember that bed-wetting is not a willful act. Children may wet the bed for different reasons, ranging from small bladders to stress, but they don't wet on purpose and shouldn't be punished.
3. Stressful events may trigger bed-wetting, even in a child who has already licked the problem once. Remember that if you make your child feel guilty or ashamed you are only compounding the problem by generating more stress, which may actually contribute to bed-wetting.
4. Don't compare your children. There are different causes for bed-wetting, and boys tend to toilet train later than girls.
5. Don't allow siblings to ridicule or tease the bed-wetter or threaten to tell others at school about the problem.
6. Arrange for a visit to the doctor to rule out physical problems. The doctor may ask about pain during urination, blood in the urine, how many accidents the child has each night, details about sleeping patterns, family history of bed-wetting, and what you have done so far to control the problem. These are routine questions.

7. During the day, get your child to practice holding the urine as long as possible to stretch the bladder. Waiting an extra ten or fifteen minutes can help the child hold urine at night long enough to awaken from a deep sleep.

8. Limit drinks in the evening and give the child some salty snacks, like pretzels, to retain water in the body.

9. Encourage your child to get up during the night to use the bathroom. Leave a nightlight on in the bathroom or a potty chair next to the child's bed.

10. Set an alarm clock to help your child assume responsibility for getting up during the night to use the toilet. Set the clock for three or four hours after bedtime. Put the clock within easy reach and show the child how to use it. Praise your child for getting up, even if the child isn't dry in the morning.

11. Tell your child that if he or she awakens and feels urine leaking out, it is time to hurry to the bathroom to see if any urine is left in the bladder.

12. If the child awakens after wetting, he or she should get up and change into dry pajamas, which should be kept next to the bed. The child should place a dry towel on the wet area of the bed.

13. Establish a routine for morning clean-up which involves the child. For example, older children can strip the bed and throw bedding and pajamas into the washer themselves.

14. Protect the mattress with a plastic cover so that odor doesn't become a problem.

15. Leave the bed open to the air during the day.

16. Insist that the child shower or bathe before school so that he or she won't smell and be teased at school.

17. If your child is eight or older, your doctor may prescribe bed-wetting alarms, which are sensitive to a few drops of urine. They awaken the child to use the toilet. Although they may take up to sixteen weeks to work, alarms can condition the child to either awaken before urinating or squeeze the muscles during sleep to prevent releasing urine.

18. Some doctors prescribe drugs to prevent bed-wetting. Although they may work, the drawback is that after their use is stopped, the problem usually returns. Also, if you are using drugs, be sure you keep them out of reach so that your child doesn't take an overdose.

OTHER COMMENTS OR SUGGESTIONS:

FAMILY ACTION PLAN: (List suggestion numbers of particular relevance and specific actions planned)

Copyright ©1999 by Barbara Kuczen. Published by
www.activeparenting.com

Blaming others   Pass-Along-Paper 7

✎ *Description of the problem:* The child does not accept responsibility for problems or failures and blames other persons, things, or situations.

✎ *Factors influencing the problem:* A child will blame others as a way to protect his or her own self concept. Blaming someone or something means that the child doesn't have to own up to a personal inadequacy. Children use coping strategies that work for them. If blaming others proves an effective way for your child to escape punishment, save face, or reduce the expectations others have for him or her then your child will continue to blame others. How you handle this problem will determine whether or not your child uses blaming others as a frequent coping strategy.

✎ *Suggestions:*
1. Check out the facts to see if the child's claim is accurate. Is there someone or something that is causing your child to experience difficulty or to fail?
2. If you are unsure as to the accuracy of your child's claims, it is better not to accuse the child of lying or making excuses. If the child is telling the truth and you doubt the story, you only rub salt into the wound.
3. Be certain that the responsibilities and expectations for your child are developmentally appropriate. Maybe your child feels compelled to blame others because he or she has absolutely no chance of success.
4. Don't make punishment so harsh that your child blames others in an attempt to escape the severe consequences of misbehavior or failure to meet a responsibility.
5. Don't modify your expectations after your child blames someone or something for his or her problems in meeting those expectations.
6. Hear your child out when the child places the blame elsewhere, but then make it clear that the consequences for the inappropriate behavior or failure to live up to a responsibility remain unchanged.
7. Make certain that your child understands how to complete an assignment or perform a task. Inability to correctly complete an activity can generate a fear of failure that drives the child to blame others.
8. Make it possible for your child to succeed by providing your child with enough time and enough materials to accomplish the task.
9. Help your child break down an overwhelming task into small steps and set up a realistic schedule for completing each phase.
10. Encourage your child to seek help if the going gets rough, rather than blaming others for problems encountered.
11. When you child does blame others, you might want to point out the inconsistencies in the logic. For example, you might say, "You blame your brother for trampling the flowers, but I saw you chase your ball into the garden three times." or "You blame your coach for not making you a starter on the team, but are you really one of the best players?"
12. Don't force your child to lie, make excuses, or blame others by reacting severely. Instead encourage open communication by sympathetically supporting your child's efforts to work through problems openly expressed.

13. The consequences for falsely blaming someone else should be worse than the consequences for admitting a problem or experiencing a failure and owning up to it.

14. Make certain that your child knows exactly what is expected of him or her. Encourage the child to make written notes and repeat directions back to you.

OTHER COMMENTS OR SUGGESTIONS:

FAMILY ACTION PLAN: (List suggestion numbers of particular relevance and specific actions planned)

Crisis coping

Pass-Along-Paper 8

✏️ *Description of the problem:* Every family experiences crises. During a crisis, stress levels reach a high. Panic is the first reaction in many people. Children who have experienced a crisis sometimes experience persistent disaster-related fears and may also react with a refusal to return to school and "clinging" behavior. At home they may stick close to a parent. Other children may withdraw from their family and friends and act listless and depressed. A child may be preoccupied with thoughts of the crisis or disaster and unable to concentrate. Sometimes the child misbehaves in school or at home or develops physical complaints such as stomachaches, headaches, or dizziness for which no medical cause can be found. Sleep disturbances are common, with the child having nightmares or reverting to bed-wetting (*See Pass-Along-Papers 5 and 6*). The child's long-term reaction will depend on the seriousness of the crisis. Age will also be a factor. Young children are more likely to refuse to attend school, while adolescents may seem tough, but act out more and show a decline in school performance. One of the most important factors will be the parents' reaction to the crisis.

✏️ *Factors influencing the problem:* When any family member is facing a crisis, the reaction usually spreads rapidly to all other members. For example, if one of the parents faces unemployment, layoff, or reduced work week, the children will hear the parents worriedly discussing their financial condition and usually react adversely. If your family has financial, or any other kind of problems, discuss the matter as a group. Children accept financial restraints more readily when they realize the reasons for them. The same will hold true for any other sacrifices the children might have to make while the family works through a crisis. In addition, if children do hear you talking, they will probably jump to conclusions and think the situation is worse than it actually is. Family problems can help your child develop important coping skills. Show your child you respect his or her ability to understand the problem. Get it out in the open and reduce stress for everyone concerned. Remember that your reaction to the crisis will be a model for the child. In addition to personal crisis, children are bombarded by the media accounts of societal crisis. For example, crime is on the increase, and virtually everyone knows someone who has had a burglary or robbery, or otherwise been the victim of crime. Children are basically trusting, and the firsthand realization that people do commit crimes in real life, and not just on television or in the movies, is stress-producing. It may be difficult for you to reassure your child when you are experiencing identical fears, but again your model of calm coping can help steady the child. If you have a burglary or are otherwise victimized, talk out the feelings of anger, fear, and humiliation. A crisis is truly the test of fire when it comes to coping. Children who are able to look back and see they were effective in handling their stress come away from the crisis stronger than ever.

✏️ *Suggestions:*

1. When facing a crisis, your first reaction is usually your worst. Panic will only prolong the stress reaction and does nothing to resolve the situation. If you panic, your child will probably become more upset.
2. You and your child must ultimately cope with any crisis. You can't avoid it. Coping usually takes the form of some type of adaptation, or change. Once you realize that making an adjustment is required, it will become easier to discuss what should be done.
3. If possible, deal with resolving one crisis at a time, rather than becoming confused by simultaneously anguishing over several at once. Work as a family to set priorities.

4. Try to move through the crisis as quickly as possible, arriving at a carefully conceived coping plan. Involve your child in making this plan.
5. Don't listen to rumors, and advise your child to do likewise.
6. Realize that adults and children differ in their reactions to a crisis.
7. If you or your child are already under high levels of stress, your reactions will be more severe than if you were unstressed prior to the crisis.
8. Realize that your attitude about accepting challenges will determine your reaction. If you respond in a positive fashion, you provide an upbeat model for your child.
9. Get support and help for you and for your child if necessary!
10. Research shows that those who manage to confide in someone - a friend, a relative, a counselor - do better in a crisis. Encourage your child to confide in you.
11. Guard against becoming so overwhelmed in your own struggles that you fail to notice your child's struggles.
12. Model a "take charge" attitude so that you and your child come through the crisis healthier and stronger than before, but don't be afraid to also express your grief.
13. When you talk to your child, don't falsely minimize the seriousness of what has happened. Honestly discuss the crisis and make positive plans for the future.
14. Reassure your child that the family will stay together. Your child's fear of separation may be intensified as a result of the crisis.
15. Let your child know that the most important things in life are still intact. You still have each other.
16. Get back to your daily routine as quickly as possible. Celebrate a birthday, follow the same holiday or bedtime rituals, eat dinner at the same time.
17. Try not to involve your child in stressful activities, such as waiting endlessly in the waiting room for the results of a relative's surgery.
18. Recognize that healing takes time and that your child's symptoms of stress will probably disappear on their own when life gets back to normal. If they don't seek professional help.

OTHER COMMENTS OR SUGGESTIONS:

FAMILY ACTION PLAN: (List suggestion numbers of particular relevance and specific actions planned)

Copyright ©1999 by Barbara Kuczen. Published by

Crying in Response to Stress or Frustration

Pass-Along-Paper 9

✎ *Description of the problem:* Children respond in differing ways to stress, frustration, anger, conflict, or embarrassment. It is common for younger children, in particular, to burst into tears under these circumstances. Crying can be an effective and healthy way to vent. However, the child that cries at the slightest provocation can earn the label of *cry-baby* from siblings and peers. Also, adults can grow less sympathetic over time to what they view as *crocodile tears*. If a child cries in response to injury, fear, loneliness, or extreme stress, adults should be compassionate. However, if the child is using tears to gain attention or manipulate a situation, adults must guide the child to more acceptable behavior. Giving the child attention or satisfying his or her demands will only reinforce crying as a method of responding to stress. Obviously, your child's age will largely determine your expectations.

✎ *Factors influencing the problem:* Children tend to resort to stress management techniques that work for them. If you pay attention to the child's crying, give in to his or her demands, or offer attractive alternatives or treats to stop the tears, the child discovers crying works as a way to get what you want. Ask yourself what prompts the child to begin crying. Does the child cry to get something or in order to be allowed to participate in an activity? Does the child cry in response to a verbal or physical conflict with another child? Do tears usually follow criticism by an adult or another child? Is frustration at having something taken away or not being allowed to finish an activity the stimulus? Does the child cry to avoid having to participate in an activity? It is also important to identify what times of the day the child most often cries. Is the child more likely to cry in the morning, when facing the challenges of the day ahead, or in the evening, when tired? Does he or she frequently cry during highly active times, when over-stimulated, or right before meals, when hungry. Perhaps the child cries unpredictably, at all times of the day. When the child is crying, does he or she respond to soothing or reason or just cry harder when comforted? Does the child stop as soon as he or she gets what is desired or continue to sob, no matter what is offered? The answers to these questions will help you find the best ways to respond to your child's tears.

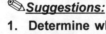

✎ *Suggestions:*

1. Determine why your child is crying. If he or she is injured or has a reasonable cause for tears, you will want to be more tolerant of the tears.
2. Crying is the first means of communication used by an infant to express his or her needs. As long as crying works to effectively meet needs, the child is likely to continue to cry. Teach your child alternatives to crying. The best substitute for tears is using language to express your feelings. Discuss the value of talking out a conflict, expressing angry feelings with words, or asking for adult help. The child can also walk away from a bad situation, or abide by the rules or decision.
3. Does your child have more accidents than other children? Perhaps these accidents are an intentional way of gaining attention, affection, and comfort. Give the child more attention for positive achievements.
4. Has your child only recently increased his or her episodes of crying? If so, has there been a major life change - such as a new baby in the family, move, divorce, or death that is upsetting the child? Support your child in efforts to deal with the changes.

5. When the child cries, determine the cause of the problem. If the child has a real reason for tears, help solve the problem. If the child is crying for attention or to manipulate a situation, ignore the tears. Don't make eye contact with the child or indicate through your body language that you are paying attention. At first, the child will cry louder to attract your attention, which is predictable. Don't give in by paying any attention to the child, or you will reinforce the notion that crying works. When the child stops crying, immediately approach the child to discuss the problem. If the child starts crying again, tell her or him, "We can't solve this problem until you have stopped crying." Then walk away and ignore the child until the tears stop.

6. Before going to school, the grocery store, a shopping center, a birthday party, or a friend's house, remind your child of alternatives to crying and the consequences of using tears to get your way.

7. Expect your child to react to disappointment by crying, but do not give-in, or you will reinforce crying behavior as a means to achieve an end.

8. If your child begins to cry in public, remove the child to a private location.

9. Be consistent in the way you handle your child's crying. Don't give in because others are present and you are embarrassed.

10. Don't allow your child to seek out another adult for attention or satisfaction after you have said, "No."

11. When your child is feeling angry, disappointed, or frustrated by one of your rules or decisions, explain the reasons behind it.

12. Communicate your feelings about how you respond to your child's crying to grandparents, baby-sitters, teachers, and older siblings. Ask for their cooperation.

13. Avoid situations that are overly competitive, extremely frustrating, or demanding beyond the child's maturity level.

14. Compliment your child for responding to stress without tears, letting the child know that you recognize that a situation was difficult and that the child successfully used appropriate coping techniques.

15. Realize that crying is common in younger children and appropriate when a child is hurt, lonely, afraid, or extremely upset.

OTHER COMMENTS OR SUGGESTIONS:

FAMILY ACTION PLAN: (List suggestion numbers of particular relevance and specific actions planned.)

Copyright ©1999 by Barbara Kuczen. Published by Active Parenting Publishers. www.activeparenting.com

Cursing (Swearing) — Pass-Along-Paper 10

✏️ *Description of the problem:* Children learn language by listening to those around them. Early in life, most children are exposed to cursing or swearing. Parents, other adults, siblings, or playmates say crude words, usually in anger. At first the child does not understand the literal meaning of these words, but senses that they are used in certain circumstances, with special inflection and tone. After hearing one of these words, the child decides to use it. The first time the parent or teacher hears the child use foul language, he or she usually reacts with shock or laughter, with questions about where the child learned such a word, and with strict orders never to use the word again. Other children who witness this exchange will often laugh or repeat the word. The child quickly learns that use of this undesirable language results in attention.

✏️ *Factors influencing the problem:* It is important to determine if there is a pattern to the child's cursing. What seems to trigger it? Does the child swear when angry, frustrated, acting silly, or serving as the leader? Is the cursing part of a role playing game? Does the child use foul language indiscriminately - in front of anyone, or limit its use to children? Does the child curse only in the presence of a few good friends? What happens when the child uses profanity? Does the child laugh or look to see if an adult has heard? Do adults react with shock, do other children laugh and repeat the words, or do the other children tell the child not to use such language? Is the child more likely to swear at a particular time of day or in a certain location - such as the bathroom or the playground? Understanding the factors that seem to influence the child's swearing will help the parent curb the child's tendency to use inappropriate language before this manner of speaking becomes more regular and frequent. The sooner you eliminate profanity from your child's speech, the better. Swearing can become an established bad habit.

✏️ *Suggestions:*

1. Remember that children model the language they hear. If you curse, your child will repeat these words. Make it clear to older siblings in the family that younger children are likely to repeat foul language heard in the home. The older children have a responsibility to model appropriate language and behavior.
2. Do not respond with undue attention to a child's use of profanity. Avoid laughter or surprise and instead react in a calm fashion.
3. Talk to your child with the same respect and in the same manner you expect the child to use when talking to you or to others.
4. If you have identified a pattern to the child's cursing, use this information to solve the problem. For example, if the child swears when bored, provide a stimulating activity before the child reaches the boredom level. If the child uses profanity when playing an adult role, such as a truck driver, make it clear that few adults in that occupation swear.
5. If the child tends to swear when frustrated or angry, plan in advance how the child can appropriately express these feelings the next time they arise. Encourage your child to verbally express feelings of anger, disappointment, or frustration rather than resorting to outbreaks.

6. Preschool children often go through a phase of "bathroom talk," where they like words such as *poo-poo,* or *pee-pee.* The fascination with these words is common at three- or four-years-old and is usually over after a brief phase. Parents should not overreact and give these words too much attention. Instead, adults should model correct terminology for basic body parts and functions and indicate that the use of other childish words is silly.

7. Respond consistently to the child when he or she curses. Don't laugh one day and act shocked the next.

8. Explain to the child exactly what he or she said that was inappropriate. For example, "The name you called your sister is not polite. I know you are angry with her, but you must find a better way to let her know how you feel."

9. Decide in advance on an appropriate consequence for each incidence of swearing and follow it consistently. For example, each time the child curses, the child might have to leave the company of others and sit alone for five minutes.

10. Enlist the help of teachers, babysitters, and relatives in consistently following through with techniques you are using to eliminate cursing.

11. Monitor those situations in which your child is likely to "go off", and redirect the child if necessary.

12. Monitor the behavior of siblings and friends so that they don't taunt or tease the child to deliberately provoke a reaction.

13. Teach the child to talk it out, walk away, or ask an adult to help if the child feels that he or she is losing control.

14. Prior to those situations you have identified as potential triggers for your child (e.g. going to a party, visiting a friend, or going to the bathroom), remind him or her of the rules and the consequences for breaking them.

15. Tell playmates the rules for appropriate behavior and language in your home.

16. Remind your child that other parents will not approve of cursing. Tell the child he or she may be embarrassed, not allowed to play with the friend, or visit at the friend's house if the parents hear bad language.

17. Teach your child socially acceptable alternatives to curse words for expressing irritation, frustration, or anger - words such as *darn* or *heck*.

18. Limit your child's exposure to television programming, movies, and song lyrics which model profanity.

19. When you and your child hear profanity, indicate your disapproval to your child.

20. Teach your child to monitor his or her own stress levels to determine if a loss of control is likely.

21. Provide a quiet area for your child to retreat to when the child senses that he or she is losing control.

22. Praise your child when you see her or him using appropriate means for handling anger, disappointment, or frustration.

OTHER COMMENTS OR SUGGESTIONS:

FAMILY ACTION PLAN: (List suggestion numbers of particular relevance and specific actions planned.)

Death

Pass-Along-Paper 11

✎*Description of the problem*: Children have a natural, healthy curiosity about death. Yet, many parents are taken completely off guard when a child says, "Mommy, I am afraid you are going to die and leave me," or "Daddy, am I going to die?" The mere thought of a child dying, or a parent dying and leaving the child, is so stress-producing that many parents react with anxiety or try to avoid further discussion. The child may become more upset or frightened by the parent's reaction than by an honest discussion of death. If parents aren't candid on the subject, the child is forced to rely on other sources of information—namely friends and the media. Many young children develop a distorted view of death from television. They see an actor die on one show, only to find the performer alive and well on the next program. Television has caused some children to associate death with violence. When they are told of a death, they automatically ask, "Who killed him?" Following a death, it is important that the child accepts and works through his or her grief in order to avoid later emotional and behavioral problems.

✎*Factors influencing the problem:* The child's prior experience with death, developmental level, and emotional maturity will affect his or her response to the loss. Young children under the age of four have difficulty comprehending the meaning and finality of death and often equate it to the cycle of sleep. It is not until the age of five- or six-years-old that children begin to realize that when someone dies they don't come back. At about the age of nine, the child realizes that death is part of the inevitable biological process and that anyone - not merely the aged - can die. Of course, the strength of the bond between the child and the deceased will play a large part in determining the intensity of the grief.   When families face the death of someone near and dear, it is difficult to avoid the issue. At this point parents are facing double stress. Not only must they cope with their own grief, but also must explain to their children what happened. However, adults should keep in mind that they provide a model for coping and expressing grief.

✎*Suggestions:*

1. Don't wait for your child's life to be touched by death to deal with it. Use the natural life cycle of plants and animals to discuss the transition from birth to death. Use the death of a small mammal or fish to teach about burial. Accept your child's curiosity about death as natural and healthy. Don't be shocked if the child asks probing questions, such as how someone looks after death, or wants to see or touch a dead pet. Openly discuss death. In the event of death, don't hesitate to communicate your grief or sense of loss.
2. Encourage your child to talk about personal feelings. Explain that it is natural for children to experience a fear of death. Tell the child that you know how it feels to worry about death or to grieve after a death. However don't force a child to talk if the child is not ready.
3. Don't offer explanations of death that confuse the child. For example, telling the child that "God took Grandma" can make the child angry with the Lord. Saying "Grandma went for a long sleep" may make the child fear bedtime. Some mental health professionals   believe that telling a child "Grandma went on a long trip" may make the child wonder why Grandma deserted them without even saying good-bye. Ultimately, the child reasons that it must be because he or she was bad.

4. Don't shelter your child from death. Allow the child to experience the loss and grief, and tell your child you are feeling it too. A reasonable period of mourning is important for everyone. Don't rush out and replace your child's dead pet with an adorable puppy or immediately distract the child from the sorrow of losing a loved one by arranging a vacation. For example, one young lady who lost her mother at five years old grew into a guilt-ridden teen who said, "I must have been an awful person. You know I never even cried when my own mother died!" Solicitous relatives provided the young girl with one diversion after another, and the child never experienced the normal grief until she was a teenager.

5. Don't be upset if your young child doesn't show grief at the loss of someone close. Children under the age of five or six really don't comprehend the finality of death. Many young children keep the relationship alive by fantasizing, and may not understand the loss for months. In the death of a mother or father, reality only hits some children when the surviving parent begins dating again. Gently remind the child over and over again about what has happened until it finally sinks in. Let the child know where the body is buried and visit the grave. Keep in mind that it is normal for children to have a shorter period of sadness than adults.

6. During times of mourning, children rarely find the comfort in religion experienced by adults. In fact, some children become confused when told: "Uncle Paul was a very good man. God took him up to heaven." They wonder how wise it is to be "good." It is normal for children to sometimes become angry at the deceased for leaving.

7. Realize that your child may fantasize about death by role-playing a death, discussing how he or she would cope with the death of a parent, or speculating about life in the hereafter.

8. Avoid being hard-boiled or overly clinical about death. Children need reassurance that the likelihood of a parent's death is remote. Often questions about death are really their way of asking, "Who will take care of me?"

9. Allow young children to attend funeral services if they want to, provided the service will not be extremely emotional and the child will be cared for by an adult not experiencing intense grief.

10. In the case of a terminal illness, prepare the child by talking about the seriousness of the illness and the possibility of death.

11. Since young children are egocentric, make it clear that the child had nothing to do with causing a death. Let the child know you cannot "wish" a person to death, nor does misbehaving cause someone to die.

12. Watch for the warning signs of stress. (See *Pass-Along-Paper* #44)

OTHER COMMENTS OR SUGGESTIONS:

FAMILY ACTION PLAN: (List suggestion numbers of particular relevance and specific actions planned)

Copyright ©1999 by Barbara Kuczen. Published by

Defiant behavior

Pass-Along-Paper 12

✏️ *Description of the problem:* Defiant behavior is also called noncompliance or disobedience. It occurs when the child refuses to comply with reasonable rules and expectations. This problem may be the most common source of referral for professional help. Defiant behavior peeks during the *terrible twos* and then usually diminishes. During the adolescence years, children can become very negative. Experts have identified three types of disobedient or noncompliant behavior. During the *terrible twos* the child may respond to your demands by doing exactly the opposite of what you said. A second form of disobedience occurs when the child throws a temper tantrum or announces angrily, "I won't, and you can't make me!" The third type of defiant behavior involves passive resistance, in which the child whines, complains, pouts, delays, or sulks when asked to do something. A certain amount of noncompliance is considered normal as the child struggles to establish independence. However, if your child develops a pattern of resisting most rules or demands and does so with great intensity, a problem exists.

✏️ *Factors influencing the problem:* Inconsistency on the part of adults is probably the greatest cause for defiant behavior. Many of the demands that are made are unpleasant. It is not fun to pick up your toys, go to bed, or take out the garbage. It is perfectly normal to try to get out of doing the unpleasant. If adults back down on their demands, it teaches the child that resistance works and he or she is likely to resist again in the future. Sometimes the parents cannot agree on rules and standards for behavior, which forces the child to disobey one or the other. Some parents set goals and expectations so high that the child is doomed to failure. The child comes to view the parents as unreasonable and therefore feels justified in defying them. An overly critical, nagging parent can have the same effect on a child. Sometimes the parents provide an adult model of noncompliance. They express contempt for the law and for others, which the child begins to model. Of course when children are tired, hungry, sick, or stressed they are more likely to disobey.

✏️ *Suggestions:*

1. Involve your child in establishing rules. Make certain that they are clear, simply stated, and well-understood. Above all, be careful about having too many rules. Many children will try to comply if they think the rules are reasonable, but will become defiant if too many demands or limitations are placed upon them.
2. Consider the child's developmental level when making rules or setting expectations. Are they reasonable?
3. Try to explain your rules and expectations to your child from the child's own perspective. If he or she questions one of your demands never explain by saying, "Because I said so!" or "Because I'm the parent - that's why!"
4. Communicate your expectations for your child to grandparents and other relatives, teachers, and babysitters.
5. Don't force your child into a confrontational situation, especially if you sense that the child is tired or stressed.
6. State the rules as impersonally as possible, such as "No running is allowed in the house," rather than "I told you not to run in the house."
7. Use nonverbal techniques for helping the child to obey. If you have said, "It's time to put away the blocks ," and the child is still building, walk over and help to put them away.

8. State your demands in positive terms. Rather than saying, "Stop running!" say "It's time to walk."
9. Be calm and businesslike when you remind your child of the rules. Don't get angry or take the child's noncompliance personally or as a sign of poor parenting.
10. Make the punishment fit the crime. Don't engage in harsh discipline but instead make the consequence a logical outcome of the behavior - for example, "If you blow bubbles in the house, you can't have the bubbles."
11. Time-out sometimes works when the child is acting defiant. Say, "I can see you are under some stress. Please go to your room until you feel better and are ready to follow the rules."
12. Don't call out demands from another room. Make eye contact with your child to be sure that the child heard and understood exactly what is expected. Have the child repeat back what you said.
13. Remember that total compliance is not your goal. Reasonable questioning of authority and a certain amount of healthy assertiveness is a sign of independence.
14. Recognize that children differ in temperament and some are more likely to demonstrate defiant behavior. It is not your fault, nor the fault of the child's, but it makes your job more challenging. Repeated defiance can become a habit and create problems later in life.

OTHER COMMENTS OR SUGGESTIONS:

 **FAMILY ACTION PLAN:** (List suggestion numbers of particular relevance and specific actions planned)

Copyright ©1999 by Barbara Kuczen. Published by

Discipline

Pass-Along-Paper 13

✏️ *Description of the problem:* According to experts, children misbehave to accomplish certain goals. They might want attention, a feeling of power, or revenge. Sometimes they act helpless and inadequate when they are feeling discouraged. Adults often label actions as misbehavior, when actually they are the result of a child being sick, tired, hungry, or frustrated. In other cases, inappropriate conduct may be caused by a child's curiosity, desire to be helpful, or ignorance of the rules or customs. Remember that all troublesome behavior is not misbehavior. Next, if the child is misbehaving, try to pinpoint the goal of the child's misbehavior. If the intentional misbehavior works to accomplish the goal of attention, for example, the child is more likely to repeat the action in the future. How parents respond to misbehavior will determine whether it is used in the future to achieve goals. If you believe that the child seeks attention, redirect the child and provide the needed attention for positive behavior. If the child displays inadequacy, remember that he or she is trying to tell you not to expect too much. The child is discouraged. Don't give up and do things for the child and avoid criticizing the child. Instead, focus on small accomplishments and efforts.

✏️ *Factors influencing the problem:* Optimally, discipline should help children gain in self-control. It should not be an attempt by the parent to control or punish. Therefore, discipline should follow as a logical outcome of the behavior in question. For example, the child who runs through the flower garden, destroying the plants, might be asked to pay for their replacement and help in the planting or be assigned some other yard work. In dealing with discipline matters, you should attempt to determine the cause for the problem. It might be that demands made were beyond the child's level or capacity, which would justify a change in adult behavior—rather than the child's. Many parents have found that they get better results by encouraging and reinforcing good behavior, rather than focusing on bad. Although at times misbehavior can't be ignored, the techniques that follow involve an overall positive philosophy.

✏️ *Suggestions:*
1. Avoid confrontations by sensing when your child is under stress or approaching the frustration level.
2. If you sense a squabble is about to turn into a brawl, step in and guide the children in working through their problem (but wait until the last minute, in order to give them a chance at problem-solving).
3. If you elect to use punishment, dispense it as soon after the misbehavior as possible. No waiting "till your father gets home."
4. Help young children, in particular, interpret the impact of their actions on others. Since they are basically self-centered, young children rarely deal with the full implications of a behavior.
5. Remove temptations from the child's environment.
6. Let children know what is expected of them, when, and why.
7. Be prepared for unusual situations where discipline might be a problem—such as a trip to the doctor's office or a plane flight. Carry entertaining items with you.
8. Keep an eye on what is happening. Don't leave children entirely on their own for long periods of time.
9. Distract or redirect young children from the problem that you see brewing.
10. Occasionally ignore a mistake or remark that "just slipped out." Never ignore the child.
11. Give children the option for a "time-out." If a child is visibly upset, tell the child you are happy to discuss it or the child can think about the problem in privacy and rejoin the group whenever she or he chooses. However, hostility, tantrums, disruptions, or disrespect will not be accepted.

12. Don't let a child do something self-destructive. Step in and offer some coping suggestions.
13. Provide a cool-down period right before bed. Limit stimulation and activity.
14. Don't expect children to stop immediately when an adult is tired of a rowdy game and says, "That's enough."
15. Involve the whole family in understanding and setting rules. Ask for discipline suggestions from children. Enforce the rules once they are set.
16. Don't ignore a source of misbehavior one day and discipline the child for the same action the next.
17. Don't make threats unless you fully intend to carry them through. Your discipline will become meaningless or invite testing.
18. Don't be afraid to apologize if you are wrong, lose your temper, or are unduly brutal with a tongue-lashing.
19. Never force a child to read or to learn as a punishment. The potential damage to learning motivation is obvious.

OTHER COMMENTS OR SUGGESTIONS:

FAMILY ACTION PLAN: (List suggestion numbers of particular relevance and specific actions planned)

Copyright ©1999 by Barbara Kuczen. Published by

Divorce   Pass-Along-Paper 14

✎ *Description of the problem:* Divorce doesn't have to devastate your child. Undoubtedly, divorce is tremendously stress-producing for parents and children. It is probably one of the most traumatic experiences in life. Nonetheless, it doesn't doom a child to a lifetime of unhappiness and poor adjustment. Parents who can shake the usual guilt feelings and face the challenge of making it through the difficult "mourning period" can help their children establish emotional stability and acquire new coping skills in the process.

✎ *Factors influencing the problem*: Studies show that less than ten percent of children affected by divorce think it was for the best. Despite the tension and problems, they wish their parents had stayed together. Most children feel alone in facing their parents' divorce. It doesn't matter how many friends have gone through the process or how widespread the phenomenon. The child feels forsaken and worries about being left with no one to provide care. Life has suddenly become unpredictable. The child questions just who can be counted on and wonders if she or he will lose the parents' love. The child longs for the happy days gone by and may become depressed or burst into tears without the slightest provocation. Schoolwork can be affected as the child grows restless, is unable to concentrate, or fails to find any relevance in academic studies. Who cares about reading when one's parents have just gotten divorced? Some children become physically ill, and it is common for children to become aggressive and irritable. Or they may try to act indifferent, deny the whole mess, or become angry at their parents. Yet parents are also experiencing profound levels of stress. In some cases the new arrangements mean there is less time to spend with the child. Some children sense their parents' distressed condition and end up worrying more about them than their parents do about the children. Following are some suggestions for coping with the stress of divorce. Many are difficult to implement. However, handling the tumultuous short-term aftershocks of divorce can minimize long-term stress for you and your child.

✎ *Suggestions:*
1. Recognize that mother, father, and family life are the most important components of your child's life. The stress of divorce is understandable and unavoidable.
2. Don't try to hide the fact that there has been a separation. Your child will probably experience more stress from the anxiety of not knowing what is happening than in learning the truth. Even if you are successful in hiding the fact, when the child finds out he or she may feel cheated or tricked and lose trust in you.
3. Preserve your child's love and respect for the other parent. When a marriage fails, parents often feel guilty and magnify their mate's faults in order to place the blame elsewhere.
4. Don't go into detail about the reasons for the divorce. Merely say you were no longer happy together.
5. Don't try to convince your child (or anyone else) that the whole thing is not your fault.
6. Don't get upset when your child begins to recount all the other parent's good points.
7. Try not to expose your child to bickering, arguments, or long periods of silence. Don't allow your child to get involved in arguments or take sides.
8. Never allow your child to think for a moment that she or he was the cause for the divorce. Make it clear that no child ever causes a divorce. It is between adults. Children are egocentric and tend to place themselves in the middle of everything. Don't let your child think that "Daddy left because I was bad."
9. Be sure both parents give the child an outpouring of love, affection, and reassurance.

10. Don't make the child feel that the divorce has placed impossible responsibilities on her or him by making comments such as, "You're the head of the house now" or "You're all I have left."

11. Spend more time listening to your child. Encourage the child to express feelings. Emphasize that it is natural to feel anger, fear, and sadness. Let the child know that sometimes there may be a feeling of wanting to be with the other parent. Tell your child that whenever feelings start to build up, it is time to talk about them. Allow him or her to freely telephone the other parent.

12. Don't let your child harbor false hope that you will all get together again. Although children often fantasize that it might happen, make it clear that in reality it won't.

13. Your child may develop temporary behavior problems in an effort to rebel, gain attention, or test your love.

14. Your child may regress and act more like a baby. Remember, those times were more comfortable.

15. Your child may become anxious or upset over anything that threatens security. Maintain stability in routine and relationships.

16. Don't confuse a young child's request for a "new daddy" or "new mommy" with loss of affection. The child simply wants to have a "normal" family like the other kids.

17. Some children do try to reject the absent parent and any qualities associated with that parent—such as a love for sports. The child, in turn, hates sports.

18. Don't compare your child's faults to the faults of your mate by making remarks such as "You're just like your mother!" The child may fear rejection.

19. Point out that there are many different types of families, but that they still are families. Point out specific examples of families that include two parents, only a mother, only a father, grandparents, or other relatives. Depending on your philosophy, you may want to include living-together arrangements.

20. If you move, be sure to let your child keep comfortable, familiar possessions.

21. Don't ever use your child to hurt your spouse.

22. Don't ask your child to express a preference for custody. The child is placed in a no-win situation in which any choice creates guilt for not having chosen the other parent.

23. Don't try to compensate by becoming overindulgent or allowing your child to "get away with murder."

24. Let the school know what is happening. Make plans for both parents to stay involved in school affairs.

25. If you find the school is dealing with the family in a stereotypical fashion or otherwise discriminating against single-parent families, call the matter to their attention. Few teachers intentionally hurt children.

26. Don't expect your child to have massive adjustment difficulties. Don't blame every problem the child has in the future on the divorce.

27. Make it clear that you never divorce a child. Mommy will always be Mommy, and Daddy will always be Daddy. Divorce doesn't change the love between parent and child.

OTHER COMMENTS OR SUGGESTIONS:

FAMILY ACTION PLAN: (List suggestion numbers of particular relevance and specific actions planned.)

Copyright ©1999 by Barbara Kuczen. Published by
www.activeparenting.com

Eating (overeating) Pass-Along-Paper 15

✎ *Description of the problem:* Overeating leads to obesity, or excess body fat. Fat children suffer from their obesity. Their peers poke fun at them, parents may disapprove, and studies indicate that teachers may even assign a fat child a lower grade than a thin child. Society discriminates against fat people, and fat children experience blows to the ego that scar for a lifetime. The child may become dependent on food for comfort or relief in times of stress. If the problem is severe, it can even impair gross motor development. Fat children suffer from a higher incidence of respiratory disease, high blood pressure, and cholesterol and triglycerides in the blood. They are more accident-prone and have more orthopedic ailments. Even the parent-child relationship can suffer if the fat child is constantly nagged and urged to stick to a diet.

✎ *Factors influencing the problem:* Obesity is linked to a number of differing factors. Most parents hope the problem is caused by a metabolic disorder, which is rarely the case. Some weight problems are hereditary in nature and involve the efficiency with which the body uses food and stores fat, although an inherited stocky body frame should not be confused with obesity. Temperament can also affect weight. Easygoing, relaxed individuals burn fewer calories than people with active personalities. However, of all these influences it appears that environmental conditioning is the most significant. Eating is a family affair. Researchers have even found that the pets of fat people have double the chance of being fat than the pets of thin people. Obesity is linked to attitudes and habits children begin to form in infancy. As a nation we have learned to crave sugar, salt, and spices. Estimates vary, but experts say that the average American consumes as much as 134 pounds of sugar per year. In fact, you can purchase candy in more places in this country than you can bread. Some experts feel that since sugar consumption has risen so drastically in recent years, it is taking the place of other vital and less fattening nutrients in our diet. Salt is another potentially dangerous food product. Few young children will request it, but just watch parents automatically reach for the shaker and liberally sprinkle the child's entire plate. After a time child learns to season food. You have probably heard the saying, Fat baby, fat adult. Research tends to support this statement: over eighty-five percent of all over- weight children grow up fighting a weight problem. It appears that the development of excessive fat cells may doom the child to a lifetime of weight gain from the slightest overeating. Fat cells formed in childhood may remain throughout life and quickly absorb fatty end products.

✎ *Suggestions:*
1. Monitor your child's weight. Check with the doctor to determine if the child is actually overweight.
2. Analyze when and why your child overeats. If the child eats when stressed, attempt to control the stressors and teach your child some alternatives for stress-management. Above all, the child should be able to identify when food is being used as a pacifier. If the child eats out of loneliness, help the child to arrange some outside social activities or recreational programs. If anger prompts overeating, the child should be made to realize that she or he is the only person being punished. Some children eat when fatigued. Their resistance is down, as is blood sugar. Insisting that the child eat regular, balanced meals can help prevent this situation.
3. Don't assume that a fat baby is more healthy or more appealing. The fat cells that are developing will plague your child for a lifetime.
4. Don't constantly feed an infant or use food to calm or appease a child. Don't begin a diet of varied, solid foods too early in the child's life. Consult your pediatrician.

5. Don't use food as a reward.
6. Don't urge your child to eat when the child is not hungry.
7. Don't insist that the child clean the plate.
8. Don't associate eating with achievement, by overreacting when a child eats well, eats a lot, or completely finishes a serving.
9. Don't allow your child to deal with stress by overindulging. A tasty treat might be effective for relaxation, but you should draw the line at overeating.
10, Don't serve high calorie meals or snacks. Serve fruit for dessert.
11. Don't make eating and mealtime the focal part of family life.
12. Don't celebrate with food.
13. Don't try to bolster your child's spirits with food.
14. Establish firm eating habits and try to stick to them, even on special days, at special events, in restaurants, or on vacation.
15. If the child expresses a fierce craving for something fattening, suggest that your child have a tiny portion—just to satisfy the taste buds.
16. Avoid high calorie school lunches by packing a nutritious, low-calorie lunch.
17. Serve smaller portions.
18. If you sense your child is about to overindulge, try to direct him or her to some physical activity.
19. Involve the child in any weight-reduction program. Since the child is growing, maintaining existing weight may solve the problem if the child is not extremely overweight. Older children sometimes benefit from the accountability provided by enrolling in organized weight reduction programs.
20. Younger children probably won't understand the concept of calorie reduction and can interpret being deprived of food as a withdrawal of love. Instead, provide low calorie meals and snacks. Remember, any diet must begin in the grocery store.
21. Remember that many healthy foods, such as natural nut mixes, are also fattening. There isn't much difference in calorie intake between consuming a large banana or a Hostess Ho Ho (although the fat content differs.) Check your calorie book when planning your shopping list to identify healthy, low-calorie foods.
22. Provide your child with a good model of eating and exercise. Plan to workout, jog, or walk together.

OTHER COMMENTS OR SUGGESTIONS:

FAMILY ACTION PLAN: (List suggestion numbers of particular relevance and specific actions planned)

Eating (poor)   Pass-Along-Paper 16

✎*Description of the problem:* The child eats too little or is finicky, refusing to eat or to even try many foods. The child may dawdle, play with food, attempt to hide food, slip food to the dog, or put food in the mouth but not chew it.

✎*Factors influencing the problem:* A certain amount of fussiness about food is perfectly normal in children. Also, a poor appetite might be the result of illness, stress, or unappealing food. Try to determine what specific foods your child refuses to eat and what food is enjoyed. Remember that people do not eat simply for nourishment. Meals are a social experience, a time when important learning takes place. Patterns of eating behavior begin to form during infancy. Some babies begin life as good eaters, while others are collicky and resistant during feeding. The eating behaviors observed in infancy may or may not lead to a picky preschool eater. If a parent overreacts to a child's failure to eat, the child learns that food is an excellent way to exert control or gain attention. Be careful not to beg, threaten, coax, or reward your child at mealtime. If you obviously display worry about your child's eating, he or she may get more satisfaction out of not eating than eating. The child may use eating as a means to punish or control adults. Controlling food consumption is also a means for asserting independence. By not eating, the child is in effect saying, "I am in control of my body." Many experts believe anorexia nervosa, a life threatening eating disorder, may be an attempt for an individual to gain some feeling of control over an otherwise out of control life.

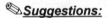

✎*Suggestions:*

1. Check with your child's doctor to rule out illness as a cause of under eating. Is stress causing a loss of appetite?
2. Make mealtime a happy, pleasant occasion. Set the table attractively, play soft music, and avoid heated arguments.
3. Involve your child in the selection and preparation of meals. Your child will be more interested in food he or she has shopped for and helped cook.
4. To make food more interesting to your child, use cookie cutters and other creative techniques, such as arranging food to make a flower.
5. Teach your child about nutrition and the importance of good eating for a happy, healthy life.
6. Be realistic about the size of the portions that you expect your child to eat.
7. Don't serve your child large helpings, which can be overwhelming.
8. Increase independence and reduce fussing by allowing your child to feel in control of his or her own eating. Serve meals family style and permit the child to serve herself or himself the type and amount of food desired.
9. Remember that children are extremely sensitive to food color, texture, and smell.
10. Some experts believe that some children may be genetically sensitive to certain foods. A child may also reject food due to food allergies.
11. Never force, ridicule, tease, or beg a child to eat.
12. Don't bribe your child with a reward for eating. The prize becomes more important than the food.
13. Encourage your child to sample foods at the beginning of the meal, when the child is still hungry. Don't insist the child finish something that he or she doesn't like. Forget the *Clean Plate Club*.
14. Discourage between meals snacking.
15. Allow a tired child to rest before sitting down to a meal.
16. Remember that some children may not like to eat because mealtime is associated with past unpleasant experiences.

17. Don't overreact to a child's eating. He or she may learn that poor eating is a good way to gain attention or exert control over parents. Guard against troubled looks or overheard worried conversations.

18. Don't judge well-being solely by the amount of food consumed. If your child appears energetic and healthy, he or she is probably eating enough.

19. Don't model under eating by starving yourself and constantly talking about your diet and your body.

20. Don't impose your own hunger and food preferences on your child, who is a unique human being and must learn to interpret her or his own body signals to eat and to stop eating.

21. Never deprive a child of food as a means of punishment.

OTHER COMMENTS OR SUGGESTIONS:

FAMILY ACTION PLAN: (List suggestion number of particular relevance and specific actions planned)

Education

Pass-Along-Paper 17

✎*Description of the problem:* The basic goal of education is not the transmittal of a body of facts and information. Instead, education is a means for assisting the child in maximizing his or her innate human potential and coping effectively with life. A good education teaches children how to teach themselves. It generates a love and enthusiasm for learning that lasts a lifetime. The self-fulfillment that results from a good education enables a child to face life's inevitable challenges with a sense of control and competency. As a parent you must be involved in providing this education for your child, and you must begin the process at birth. You cannot leave the job to the schools.

✎*Factors influencing the problem:* Recent research indicates that important brain development begins at birth, if not before. It is your job to provide a stimulating environment which supports growth, learning, and development. As you approach the job of providing a stimulating environment for your child, there are five points to remember. First, you should never force your child. Learning should be smooth and easy. If you find you are placing your child under stress because you are making demands that are too difficult, stop and reevaluate. Second, learning should be fun. If your child does not like a particular activity, try presenting it in a different manner. Third, if your child gets tired, you are no longer stimulating the child. The younger the child, the shorter the attention span. Resist the temptation to plan extended learning sessions with your child. Two shorter time periods usually work better than one long one. Don't forget to use those precious minutes while riding in the car, preparing a meal, or doing the dishes. Fourth, don't get angry or lose your temper when your child has trouble or makes mistakes. Children do not make mistakes on purpose, and they do not enjoy having trouble. If you become upset, you are generating stress for yourself and your child. If the result of your interaction is always a big blowout, with tears and angry words, your child might transfer these negative feelings to you or to learning in general. In addition, when you explode you are depriving your child of success - the fifth basic point. Success is the most important ingredient in learning. Have you ever been highly motivated to learn something - maybe chess? The interest was there, but after you got into the game, you just weren't successful at it. There's a good chance you dropped it, despite your initial enthusiasm. On the other hand, have you ever been lukewarm about learning something new, like doing a craft project. Someone encouraged you to give it a try and after starting out in a haphazard, bored manner, you began to experience some level of success. In no time at all you loved doing the craft and vowed to become an expert. Nobody likes to fail. Program attainable success into your child's life.

✎*Suggestions:*
1. Forget that old wives' tale that children should be seen, not heard. Verbal ability is closely related to success in the language arts, particularly in reading. From birth spend time encouraging your child to talk.
2. Helping your child to learn does not mean that you need to plan organized lessons. Instead, concentrate on structuring the environment so that your child learns by discovery. Real learning is the result of finding out on your own, not of being told. Get your child to talk and ask thought-provoking questions to keep the ball rolling.
3. Some parents with preschool children have an exalted notion of what educational television has to offer. They sit their child in front of the set without the slightest twinge of conscience, confident that the programming has more to offer than they do. Although the child can profit from carefully monitored TV viewing, particularly if the parent is at hand to reinforce learning, active participation of the parent in the learning process is essential.

4. Parents should begin reading to children at birth and continue through childhood. This activity transmits a love of learning and enthusiasm for reading. The key is to select material appropriate for the child's age and interests. Your librarian can help.

5. Even though you are not a trained teacher, you can help in your child's education. Your role is to provide a rich background of experiences on which formal schooling can build. For example, if your child has never visited a farm and therefore does not know what a *silo* is, what good does it do to learn how to read the word *silo*? Once your child starts school, your job is not to teach from scratch, but rather to reinforce and extend the material that is presented by the teacher. If you study the work your child brings home, you will soon see the sequence of learning. Corrected papers and homework also tell you where the child needs help. Just listening to your child read and then asking some comprehension questions can be a tremendous benefit. If you hit a snag, don't hesitate to contact the professional — your child's teacher.

6. When it comes to learning, silence is not golden. Don't mistake your child's silence for understanding. Learning is noisy and animated. Watch for that fake nod of understanding or the silent plodding along.

7. Many parents select material that is beyond the success range of their child. Maybe it is the result of wishful thinking, but the results are disastrous. Rather than challenged, your child may be defeated and unable to cope. Reading material, in particular, should be below the instructional level at school and easy enough to read with fluency and understanding.

8. There are many heated arguments about teaching reading in preschool and kindergarten. Parents should guard against forced early academics. Early education should be developmentally appropriate and include the provision of a rich background of varied experiences that help the child develop a broad vocabulary and good verbal skills.

9. Children's learning is greatly affected by a number of variables - one of which is the emotional climate in the home. If your family is experiencing unusual difficulty or grief, inform the teacher.

10. If your child doesn't see the point to an activity, it is unlikely that he or she will benefit much from doing it. Resist the "because I said so!" attitude and explain the reasons for learning.

11. Children love deserved, sincere praise. Often-repeated, meaningless words, such as *great* or *good job* have no effect. Children know when they have earned praise and when someone is patronizing them. When you offer praise, comment specifically on what you liked about the child's accomplishment.

OTHER COMMENTS OR SUGGESTIONS:

FAMILY ACTION PLAN: (List suggestion numbers of particular relevance and specific actions planned)

Copyright ©1999 by Barbara Kuczen. Published by

Fears
Pass-Along-Paper 18

✏️ *Description of the problem:* All children have fears. In fact, we often use fear to teach safety precautions. In addition to those learned by experience, others - such as fear of heights, loud sounds, or loss of balance - are instinctive. Some children develop fears that are beyond the normal range. These fears can create an overpowering panic state, a sense of dread, or an irrational aversion called a phobia. Children's fears are diverse and numerous. Common childhood fears include darkness, loud noises, monsters, animals, strangers, storms, abandonment, amusement park rides, public embarrassment, and many new situations. Between the ages of two and four, fear of thunder, darkness, animals, and strangers is common. Between the ages of four and six, the child is likely to fear imaginary creatures like ghosts and monsters. A few children continue to fear supernatural beings until they are ten years old, but more common in children ten and older is a fear of physical dangers and street violence.

✏️ *Factors influencing the problem:* Although some children seem to be born very timid, shy, and fearful, fears are often transmitted to children via adults or peers. They learn to regard a specific situation as threatening. A previous bad experience can evoke fear. A child who was bitten by a dog will probably tend to fear dogs, and maybe even furry animals in general, unless preventive action was taken after the incident. A terrifying sight on television or in the movies which was not fully understood can be a source of fear, as can an ominous warning made by an adult or a threat, such as "If you stare into the sun, your eyes will fall out." Even well-meaning reassurances such as, "There's nothing to be afraid of at school," can instill fear in a child who never thought about being afraid but wonders what you're really driving at with your remark. In addition, a parent can contribute to the problem by being overprotective or inconsistent, by making unreasonable demands or failing to provide the child with the love or attention necessary for the formation of a strong self-image. A fear is a perceived threat, and the best way to handle it is to deal with it specifically.

✏️ *Suggestions:*

1. Determine exactly what is fearful to the child. Encourage the child to talk about and explore the cause and nature of the problem. Don't take the fear lightly, ridicule, attempt coercion ("Don't be afraid, touch the birdie"), or ignore the problem. Logical explanations can help, but don't expect to explain away the fear.
2. If possible, arrange for your child to see others happy and safe in the situation he or she fears.
3. Arrange for carefully supervised contact with the fear, during which you provide positive support and understanding. This procedure is called *desensitization* and might work as follows for a child who fears birds:

Step One:	Look at pictures of birds. Discuss whether or not a bird could actually harm you.
Step Two:	Have the child hold a toy bird of some type, a plastic model, for example, or a stuffed animal.
Step Three:	Let the child watch a friend caring for and holding a pet bird.
Step Four:	Have the child watch the bird in its cage.
Step Five:	Tell the child to touch the bird briefly as the friends holds it.
Step Six:	Have the child hold the bird for five seconds with a pair of gloves on.
Step Seven:	Have the child hold the bird for ten seconds with a pair of gloves on.

Step Eight:	Have the child hold the bird for five seconds with bare hands.
Step Nine:	Hare the child hold the bird for ten seconds with bare hands.
Step Ten:	Have the child hold the bird in his or her lap and pet it.

4. Stay away from flooding therapy, in which the child is suddenly thrust into the situation feared.

5. In the case of irrational fears, such as fear of the dark, acknowledge the child's feelings but guard against adding fuel to the fire by giving credibility to the fears. For example, if the child is afraid of a monster hiding in the bedroom, ringing a bell to chase the monster out would reinforce the fear. Instead, talking about the fear, conducting a reassuring search, and leaving on a night-light can ease the child's tension.

6. It is important to provide comfort without overdoing it. Over-comforting the child with too much attention or too many hugs and kisses can lead to the belief that there is actually something to fear.

7. Some children enjoy the comforting so much that they begin responding with fear for the attention they get.

8. Provide opportunities for success and build self image, independence and responsibility which will make the child more self-assured *(See Pass-Along-Papers 35, 24, and 33.)*

9. Don't model fear to your child. A parent or sibling who is terrified of spiders will probably pass that fear on to others.

10. An overly restrictive, demanding environment can cause a child to fear authority and doubt his or her own ability to handle difficult situations - making the child fearful of those situations.

11. Rehearse in advance how the child will handle a fearful situation. Decide on positive self-talk and methods for dealing with the worst possible case (which, you should point out, is unlikely to happen.)

12. Reward your child for showing bravery and overcoming fears.

OTHER COMMENTS OR SUGGESTIONS:

FAMILY ACTION PLAN: (List suggestion numbers of particular relevance and specific actions planned)

Copyright ©1999 by Barbara Kuczen. Published by

Friends
Pass-Along-Paper 19

✎ *Description of the problem:* Friendships are a natural, healthy part of life. However, some children lack the self-confidence to make friends or have such a poor self-image that they are sure no one will like them. Unkind behavior usually signals that a child's self esteem is weak. Inflicting hurt gives a temporary feeling of power, but ultimately results in lost friendships. Patterns of friendship may vary among children, with some children preferring a large number of friends, and others having fewer, more intense relationships. Either way is fine, as long as the child does have some friends.

✎ *Factors influencing the problem:* Children need an opportunity to practice friendship. If you have an only child or a preschool child, arrange for friends to visit, or consider enrolling the child in some type of lessons or play group. If your child is school-aged and friendless, there is a problem. Don't let the child fool you by insisting, "I don't want to play with the other kids. I'd rather be by myself." While it is true that everyone enjoys being alone at times, a friendless child is an unhappy child. Talk to your child's teacher and try to get to the root of the problem so that you can plan how to solve it. Children have to learn how to be a good friend. They sense it has something to do with being kind and loyal and having fun together, but parents can offer more specific suggestions.

✎ *Suggestions:*

1. Tell your child that everyone likes to hear good things about themselves, so it's a good idea to tell your friends what you like about them and the things they do well.
2. Advise your child not to say bad things about people just to make yourself feel better. Explain that even if the person you are talking about isn't your friend, the friend you are gossiping with may think you'd do the same to him or her. Tell your child to try to say only good things. You never hurt anyone that way, and more people will like you.
3. Remind your child of how much he or she likes it when someone listens to her or him. It makes you feel important. Your child should understand that when you listen to your friends, it makes them feel important, too.
4. Warn your child about making promises. They are too easy to break, which can cost a friendship.
5. If your child isn't sure that he or she can keep a secret, then it is better to tell a friend not to tell you. Point out that if your child tells just one person, and that person tells just one person, and so on, and so on....just think of how many people will know.
6. Your child should realize that almost no one can keep a secret. If you tell your friend an important secret, lots of people will probably end up knowing your business.
7. Your child should understand the importance of sharing with friends and treating them with courtesy.
8. Don't allow your child to exclude certain children from play activities. Everyone can have fun together.
9. Your child should understand that if friends hurt your feelings or are mean, it is time to stand up for your rights or don't play with them.
10. Point out that no one can hurt your feelings unless you let them.
11. Tell your child that the best way to handle an argument is to avoid it, if possible.
12. When your child is angry with a friend, tell her or him to tell the friend exactly what the problem is. Advise your child to be calm, not to call names, or bring up old fights.

13. Your child should understand the importance of giving a friend a chance to speak his or her mind. Tell your child to listen carefully to what is being said. If your friend brings up something that happened a long time ago, advise your child to reply that that isn't part of this argument.
14. Emphasize the importance of admitting you are wrong as soon as you realize it.
15. Help your child find solutions to problems with friends that make everyone happy.
16. Tell your child that if a friend says, "I'm sorry," it's a good idea to accept the apology quickly and go on with your play.
17. If your child parts from a friend angry, suggest that the next time they meet it might be a good idea to try smiling and saying, "Hi!" The friend probably wants to forget the whole thing, too.
18. If a friend won't talk to your child, help her or him find someone else to play with rather than moping around.
19. Do not emphasize competition among friends.
20. Allow your child to select his or her own friends and play as long as everyone is getting along. Intervene when fights or squabbles occur.
21. Teach your child some temper controlling techniques, such as taking a deep breath and counting to three, or saying the alphabet.

OTHER COMMENTS OR SUGGESTIONS:

FAMILY ACTION PLAN: (List suggestion numbers of particular relevance and specific actions planned.)

Copyright ©1999 by Barbara Kuczen. Published by Active Parenting Publishers. www.activeparenting.com

Gifted child   Pass-Along-Paper 20

Description of the problem: It's difficult to imagine how being gifted could result in any problems. However, parents are often concerned about how to identify if their child is truly gifted and how to best meet a gifted child's special needs. Gifted children, as well, can experience some special stresses. There is an image of the bright or talented child as being a bookworm, with no friends and limited interests. Although they are susceptible to some special stresses, gifted children overall are just as active in extracurricular activities as their classmates. They have more hobbies and a wider range of interests. In addition, research indicates that they have fewer illnesses and are taller, better coordinated, and have greater physical endurance. Gifted children are popular with their classmates and have an excellent sense of humor. On the average they cause fewer problems at school or home and are more independent. They are less likely to cheat, steal, or take advantage of people. Gifted children are sensitive to others and better able to cope with stress. They seem almost too good to be true! But wait, all these positive statements refer only to the hypothetical, average gifted child. On an individual level, giftedness can cause your child some problems.

Factors influencing the problem: Don't assume that gifted children can fend for themselves. They need guidance and assistance, the same as other children. If your child is enrolled in a program for the gifted, development of capability is probably the major objective, with secondary attention given to emotional or coping problems. More than half of the gifted children in this country don't attend any special program, and some regular classroom teachers are ill equipped to tailor a curriculum to meet the needs of the gifted. Being bright doesn't guarantee achievement. As Thomas Edison said, "Genius is one percent inspiration and ninety-nine percent perspiration." For one reason or another, many gifted children are underachievers and a number ultimately drop out of high school. Creativity seems to peak at about four-years-old. Some experts believe that fading is not caused by maturation, but rather results from adult influences. Creative behavior produces stress and the child copes by stifling creativity.

Suggestions:

1. First determine if your child could be gifted. The following traits are associated with gifted children:

    Has scored over 125 on a test of intelligence
    Has special talent in a particular area, such as art, music, math or athletics
    Learns new concepts or skills easily
    Often appears to teach himself/herself something new
    Finds answers to questions with little or no assistance
    Is very self-sufficient for age level
    Has an advanced vocabulary for age level
    Has an excellent memory
    Often surprises adults with what he or she knows
    Has a longer attention span than most children of the same age
    Often prefers to work alone
    Hates to be interrupted when concentrating on an activity
    Is inquisitive and asks many questions
    Easily puts together puzzles difficult for age level
    Rapidly adjusts to change
    Expresses ideas well in speaking, writing, or both
    Complains of being bored by routines or at school
    Seems to do well in almost every activity undertaken

Has excellent reasoning ability (mentally working through situations - anticipating events three or four steps ahead)
Learned to read early or very rapidly
Has excelled academically in the past or is doing so currently

2. If your child is gifted, encourage her or him to experiment or try new approaches without fear of failure. Don't tell the child, "That's not how you are supposed to draw a house."

3. Encourage your child to ask questions and be curious. Make learning fun and an important part of play.

4. Children do not like to feel different. In an effort to be accepted by peers or parents, gifted children sometimes conceal their ability, become withdrawn, purposefully fail, or act out in school.

5. Don't make your child feel different by continuously boasting about his or her accomplishments. Over time the child may come to believe that you care more about the special ability than about the child as a person.

6. Don't allow siblings to nickname your gifted child *teacher's pet* or *the brain*.

7. Be prepared for siblings and friends who are jealous and react to your gifted child negatively or with hostility. Discuss the problem openly and honestly.

8. Don't insist that your gifted child devote more time to an active social life rather than pursue the area of special talent. Allow for child initiated activity.

9. Acknowledge your child's special ability and encourage the school to do likewise. Help the child actualize.

10. Don't expect too much from the child's special ability and place unreasonable demands on the child, which can only lead to failure. (Watch that teachers don't, either.)

11. If your child begins to get lazy, check to see if it could be caused by the slow pace of classroom instruction and frequent repetition of material the child has already mastered.

12. Some gifted children rely heavily on perfection and praise to maintain self-esteem. They become frustrated and upset when lofty goals are not realized. Let your child know you don't always have to be number one.

13. Successful coping involves dealing effectively with the entire range of humanity. Don't let your gifted child become intolerant and impatient with others they view as less bright, or assume an air of superiority.

OTHER COMMENTS OR SUGGESTIONS:

FAMILY ACTION PLAN: (List suggestion numbers of particular relevance and specific actions planned)

Copyright ©1999 by BARBARA KUCZEN. Published by
www.activeparenting.com

Hyperactivity

Pass-Along-Paper 21

✎ *Description of the problem:* Hyperactive children, as the term implies, seem to be continuously active and easily distracted. They have a very short attention span *(See Pass-Along-Paper 3)*, and may fidget, climb on furniture, or make a constant noise by tapping fingers or feet. They may engage in non-stop talking or humming. Tasks demanding total attention for even a short time period are difficult, if not impossible. This fact makes school particularly challenging for these children. Even if they do outgrow their hyperactivity between the ages of twelve and seventeen (as many do), by that time these children may be hopelessly behind in academics and suffering from a very poor self-image. Negative patterns of behavior may have become habit.

✎ *Factors influencing the problem:* For many years experts believed that hyperactivity might be the result of chemical imbalances; food allergies; vitamin deficiencies; reactions to food additives, colorations, or preservatives; or junk food or sugar. However, research findings have yielded little conclusive evidence about the cause hyperactivity. Some hyperactive children are treated with drugs to slow the impulses to the brain, but they also have serious side effects. It is important to note that boys tend to be more hyperactive than girls. In addition, activity level appears to be part of the temperament each child inherits. Some children are naturally more active from birth. Hyperactivity can be linked to a number of other problems, such as autism, blows to the head, poisoning, endocrine disturbances, and tumors (but these situations are *extremely rare*.) Hyperactivity can also be a symptom of attention deficit hyperactivity disorder (ADHD). If you are concerned that your child may suffer from ADHD consult your pediatrician and local school system.

✎ *Suggestions:*

1. Remember that preschool children are naturally active. Don't label your happy, healthy, normal, active child as *hyperactive*.
2. The following list of traits are common to hyperactive children. If your child has a large number, you may want to consult your doctor and local school system for testing or help.

Attends to everything; unable to ignore stimuli
Continuously in motion, fidgety, unable to sit still
Seems to touch everything
Short attention span, moves quickly from one activity to another, leaves projects half-completed
Distractible
Forgetful
Aggressive, hostile, irritable, or emotional
Dismantles or destroys toys
Low threshold for pain, temperature, or tickling; readily laughs or cries
Demanding, insists on things "my way"
Little self-control
Disrupts class, talks during class or teases other children
Clumsy
Impatient
Often loses things
Has a nervous habit, such as sucking on a blanket or clothing, biting or picking fingernails, or twirling hair
Accident-prone
Attempts reckless stunts

Interrupts
Talks loudly, excessively or rapidly
Panics
As a baby, appeared to have colic
As a baby, sucked thumb or pacifier
As a baby, rocked crib
As a baby, banged head when angry

3. Make certain that your child knows the rules, such as no running or yelling in the house. Consistently follow these rules. When your child is engaged in an inappropriate activity, explain exactly what is wrong. For example, say "The rest of us don't like the sound that you make when you keep banging your blocks on the table."

4. Monitor your child to see if he or she is getting too excited. If so, remove your child from the activity and settle the child. You should not get angry or upset. Your calmness will help soothe your child.

5. Avoid activities where your child tends to get overstimulated or increase your supervision of those situations (parties, games, outdoor play). Avoid highly competitive activities.

6. Maintain a consistent routine in your child's life. Set definite times for getting up, going to bed, taking a bath, watching television, etc.

7. Try to plan your child's day so that quiet activities break-up periods of high activity.

8. Allow plenty of time for transitions from one activity to the next. Announce in advance that it is almost time to take a bath or go to bed.

9. Plan for a cool-down period before bed when your child listens to a story, does a quiet activity, gets a massage, or talks about the day.

10. Have a *secret signal* you can use with your child in public to communicate that things are getting out of control. For example, you might tap your head to remind the child to stop and think or point downward to remind him or her to settle down.

11. Teach your child some calming techniques, such as stopping to take a deep breath, saying the alphabet, or counting backwards.

12. Enlist the help of relatives, teachers, and babysitters in controlling your child's hyperactivity.

13. Consistently follow the advise of professionals you have consulted.

OTHER COMMENTS OR SUGGESTIONS:

 **FAMILY ACTION PLAN:** (List suggestion numbers of particular relevance and specific actions planned.)

Copyright ©1999 by Barbara Kuczen. Published by

Impulsiveness   Pass-Along-Paper 22

✏️ *Description of the problem:* The impulsive child rushes into things in a sudden, forceful, spontaneous way. Even though the child may know the negative consequence of an action, he or she tends to respond in a hasty fashion, without thinking through the long term ramifications. The child has trouble delaying gratification and must satisfy his or her needs immediately. Frequently the first reaction is to get whatever is desired NOW! Children under the age of eight tend to be more impulsive than older children.

✏️ *Factors influencing the problem:* Some children seem to have been born impulsive. In other cases, the child acts impulsively out of fear or anxiety - with minor stresses causing the child to panic and behave without thinking. Sad, depressed children may often act impulsively in an effort to find some small pleasure - while a resilient child has enough happiness in life to be able to delay gratification. In some cases, impulsive behavior has been modeled by the parents or culture.

✏️ *Suggestions:*

1. Maintain a family life-style that is low-key and relatively stress-free. Avoid, especially, any situations that might upset the child immediately before departure for school.
2. Act as a model of organization and try to control your own impulsive behavior, if you are prone to such behavior.
3. Provide a system of fixed routines for the impulsive child. Studying, in particular, should be done in a quiet, private setting at the same time each day.
4. Break activities down into small chunks that guarantee a sense of progress and success. Don't allow the child to hop ahead, but instead insist that each step be completed correctly, in sequence.
5. Be sure your child understands what is expected. In some cases you can't be certain unless the child repeats directions back to you.
6. Your child may learn better via the visual or tactile modalities (seeing or doing), rather than the auditory (hearing). If so, use them.
7. Encourage your child to take "time-outs" when overstimulated. Be certain these breaks are not associated with punishment.
8. Don't overwhelm your child with choice. Present no more options than the child can effectively handle.
9. Avoid games or teaching techniques that create tension, such as a family spelling bee.
10. Teach your child some stress-breakers *(See Pass-Along-Paper 42)* to use when the child identifies that she or he is "out of control."
11. Gradually teach your young children to delay gratification by making the child wait for what is desired. Little by little increase the length of time the child waits.
12. Teach your child to solve problems and resolve conflicts, rather than impulsively taking what is desired from someone else or reacting in a "hot-headed" fashion.
13. Discuss with your child the consequences of impulsive behavior, such as losing friends, getting in trouble at school, or not being invited to visit friends' homes.
14. Teach your child to "self talk." For example, the child might say, "I can wait for my turn at the easel," or "I must think before I act."
15. Following an impulsive act, rehearse with the child how the situation might be handled more effectively in the future.

16. Decide on a nonverbal symbol that you can use with your impulsive child to signal her or him to think before acting. For example, you might tap your head to remind the child to think.
17. Praise your child for maintaining control and acting appropriately.
18. Consider professional help if you are unable to help your child control extemely impulsive behavior.

OTHER COMMENTS OR SUGGESTIONS:

FAMILY ACTION PLAN: (List suggestion numbers of particular relevance and specific actions planned)

Copyright ©1999 by Barbara Kuczen. Published by ACTIVE PARENTING PUBLISHERS www.activeparenting.com

Inappropriate behavior   Pass-Along-Paper 23

✎ *Description of the problem:* The child has bad manners or does not follow the rules at home, at school, or in public. The child has trouble functioning in social settings.

✎ *Factors influencing the problem:* Many times a child's inappropriate behavior is an effort to seek attention. Obviously, if this technique is reinforced by adults who give the child the attention desired, the inappropriate behavior will continue. Sometimes a behavior appears inappropriate to an adult who does not understand the child's developmental level. For example, a young preschooler simply doesn't have the eye-hand coordination to have perfect table manners. In other situations, the expectations may simply be too demanding. If a child is forced to line up in tight quarters, he or she might end up pushing due to feeling crowded. A child may also behave inappropriately because the rules are inconsistently enforced and poorly understood. If burping is funny one day, the child has trouble understanding why it is wrong the following day. Sometimes children behave inappropriately because they are sick, stressed, or over-stimulated. Too much noise and activity can cause the child to forget what is expected and behave impulsively.

✎ *Suggestions:*

1. Be certain that the child understands what is expected in various social situations.
2. Teach your child the rules for good manners, as well as the rules in various public places - such as an airplane, at school, in a restaurant, or in a movie.
3. Help your child understand that what is appropriate in one setting may not be appropriate in another. For example, you can cheer at a baseball game but not in a movie.
4. Before going out, review the rules for behavior at your destination. Anticipate any problem areas and discuss them in advance. For example, tell your child that she or he won't be able to talk in church or walk around in the airplane.
5. When your child engages in any form of inappropriate behavior, remove the child to a private location.
6. Explain exactly what was inappropriate about the behavior.
7. Insist on the same manners at home as you expect in public. For example, saying "please" and "thank you" or chewing with your mouth closed at the table.

8. Don't contribute to your child's inappropriate behavior by providing the wrong toys or food. For example, a noisy electronic game is not appropriate for church or an airplane ride. An ice cream cone is not appropriate while riding in a friend's car.

9. Have a predetermined signal you can use in public to quietly remind your child to think about rules or manners. You might tug your ear to indicate that he or she is making too much noise, pat your mouth to tell your child to eat more carefully or use the napkin, or tap your head to signal it's time to think about what is happening.

10. Ask the management at public places for a copy of the rules for conduct and show them to your child to indicate that this is serious business. Tell her or him the consequence for breaking the rules, such as not being allowed to come back to the swimming pool or the video arcade.

11. Make certain that siblings, relatives, babysitters, and teachers understand how you feel about your child behaving appropriately.

12. Don't model inappropriate behavior to your child.

OTHER COMMENTS OR SUGGESTIONS:

FAMILY ACTION PLAN: (List suggestion numbers of particular relevance and specific actions planned)

Copyright ©1999 by Barbara Kuczen. Published by Active Parenting Publishers www.activeparenting.com

Independence

Pass-Along-Paper 24

✏️ *Description of the problem:* The child has little confidence in his or her ability to succeed and is afraid of new experiences and challenges. The child may cling to parents in strange situations.

✏️ *Factors influencing the problem:* Positive self image and a sense of independence go hand in hand. It's difficult to have one without the other, and they are mutually enhancing. A child with a strong self image is self reliant and doesn't fear independent activities which build the child's self image further. Independence is a demonstration of competence, while simultaneously contributing to it. The urge for independence is evident in the two year old child who demands "I do it! I do it!" and constantly challenges the parents' authority. Overprotective or extremely controlling parents can thwart a child's natural desire for independence by restricting freedom or unconsciously limiting the environment so that independence is impossible.

✏️ *Suggestions:*

1. Provide your child with plenty of attention. Children who don't get enough attention will spend their time hovering around adults, trying to get more- instead of trying out their independence.
2. Provide a secure home base from which the child can venture out into independent activities, knowing that there is always a safe place to which to return.
3. Provide time for independence. If you are always in a rush to get your child off to school, there probably isn't adequate opportunity for the child to select clothing or pack a lunch.
4. Provide an environment that is conducive to independence. Install clothes racks at the child's level, get a stool for the sink, teach the child to use the microwave - whatever suits your life-style and the child's developmental level.
5. Provide opportunities for your child to share in planning for activities that contribute to independence. If your child is old enough, make school lunch his or her responsibility.
6. Use discipline and problem-solving techniques based on self-control and voluntary participation, rather than commands or orders.
7. Provide explanations for your requests and rules whenever possible.
8. Let younger children wander a little under controlled circumstances, such as at a large family party.
9. Let your child organize his or her own bedroom.
10. When driving in the car or traveling, pretend you don't know what to do or where to go and have your child direct you.

11. Play "What if..." Give your child hypothetical situations to handle. For example, "What if you lost your parents at the zoo," or "What if you had to call for an ambulance."

12 Don't over-organize your child's life so that there is no time for independent activity. Lessons, clubs, and athletics are important - but so is time for oneself.

13. Show that you value independent behavior by serving as a model for your child. Don't get hung up on sex roles that make you dependent on your wife to wash a shirt or on your husband to change a fuse.

14. Consider your child's age and developmental level when promoting independence.

15. Be positive and supportive of your child's attempts to strike out independently. Communicate your faith in the child's ability to succeed.

16. Provide your child with choices, such as "You can visit Grandma or Aunt Carol this week end."

17. Find activities where your child can independently experience success, which will build confidence.

18. Don't push your child into highly stressful, frightening independent activities before the child is ready.

19. Praise your child for independent actions.

OTHER COMMENTS OR SUGGESTIONS:

FAMILY ACTION PLAN: (List suggestion numbers of particular relevance and specific actions planned)

Jealousy

Pass-Along-Paper 25

✏️ *Description of the problem:* Jealousy takes many forms, ranging from sibling rivalry *(See Pass-Along-Paper 38)* to competing for the teacher's attention. A child can also be jealous of another's looks, abilities, lifestyle, or possessions. Jealousy can be expressed in many ways. The child may engage in overt hostility, such as hitting, kicking, or biting. Regressive behavior, such as bed-wetting, thumb-sucking, or attachment to a security object, is common in younger children. The child may appear to reject that which he or she wants the most (such as a lead role in the school play) or fears losing the most (such as a parent's love). A child may even cheat, lie, or steal to get what he or she is so jealous of possessing. Attention seeking is common, with behavior such as misbehaving, feigning illness, or refusing to eat. The child may direct aggressive acts, such as taunting or violence, at the source of the jealousy.

✏️ *Factors influencing the problem:* The root of jealousy is insecurity, manifested in either a fear that love will be lost or diminished, or in low self-esteem which makes the child prefer other people's abilities, looks, or belongings. In some cases, jealousy is quite understandable, as when there is obvious preferential treatment of one child over another. A gifted child, for example, may receive a larger share of adult attention, creating jealousy in siblings or classmates.

✏️ *Suggestions:*

1. The best protection against jealousy is to provide your child with a sense of love and security that is unconditional, which will also enhance the child's self concept.
2. Try to find some special time each day to spend alone with each of your children to help each one feel special and loved.
3. Help your child recognize his or her special abilities and talents. Provide opportunities to further develop in these areas.
4. Don't provide your child with a model of jealous behavior, by talking about how much you envy someone else.
5. Express your joy at the happiness and success of others. Encourage your child to do likewise.
6. Encourage your child to talk about jealous thoughts that may crop up. Help the child understand that we all have these feelings now and then.
7. Discuss the meaning of the saying, *"the grass is always greener on the other side of the fence."* Help your child understand that everyone has good and bad parts to their life. When we are jealous of someone, we often focus only on the good parts of that person's life.
8. Don't reinforce your child's jealousy by buying whatever the child envied.
9. Discourage your child from engaging in *can you top this* discussions with friends, in which he or she tries to go one better. For example, a friend says, "We are going to Disneyworld over spring break." Your child says, "That's nothing. We're going to Hawaii." Instead encourage enthusiastic responses, such as, "Boy, that's neat!"
10. Avoid overly competitive activities in which your child is likely to become jealous of the winner.
11. Don't constantly compare your child to siblings or other children and discourage the child from making such comparisons. Instead focus on personal growth and improvement.
12. Don't arrange for your child to participate in activities where he or she is at the lowest level. For example, if your child isn't truly advanced, enroll the child in beginner or intermediate tennis lessons.

13. Help your child appreciate his or her unique talents, strengths, and abilities and find activities where success is likely.
14. Don't place too much importance on appearance, clothing, or possessions.
15. Be sure to notice your child's accomplishments - both large and small - and offer compliments.

OTHER COMMENTS OR SUGGESTIONS:

FAMILY ACTION PLAN: (List suggestion numbers of particular relevance and specific actions planned)

Learning disabilities   Pass-Along-Paper 26

Description of the problem: In general, learning disabled children show no evidence of uncorrectable vision or hearing problems, although in many cases they do have difficulty in accurately receiving and processing information. They have a normal level of intelligence and are free from handicapping emotional conditions. Learning disabled children demonstrate erratic skill development. They attain in some areas, while experiencing difficulty in others. It is often not easy to diagnose the specific learning problem. Somewhere in the series of learning events that includes receiving, processing, integrating, utilizing, and communicating information there is breakdown. Diagnosis means finding that weak spot.

Factors influencing the problem: One of the biggest sources of confusion is that there is another group of children who closely resemble the learning disabled, exhibiting many of the same characteristics. There are no major physical, vision, or hearing impairments, and the emotional and social climate for learning is satisfactory. The big difference is that although the child is within the range of normal intelligence, he or she is at the lowest end of this range. Slow learners, as they have been termed, experience difficulty learning and achieving. Actually they are performing at a level consistent with ability. If your child is a slow learner but diagnosed as learning disabled, goals and expectations may never be reached, and the child experiences constant failure. On the other hand, a learning disabled child incorrectly classified as a slow learner will probably stay a slow learner since we tend to get what we expect from children.

Suggestions:

1. Recognize that the slow learner is consistently slow, while the learning disabled child shows a highly uneven pattern of skill development.
2. Slow learners are usually not as prone to impulsive behavior and hold onto a skill once it is learned, while a disabled learner is often highly active and apt to forget or regress.
3. Intelligence tests alone cannot be used to make a diagnosis, since many learning disabled children do poorly on these tests.
4. If you suspect that your child has a problem, check with your pediatrician, who will probably arrange for a complete physical, vision and hearing tests, blood and urine analysis, and whatever else is indicated.
5. The following are *possible* symptoms of learning disabilities:

    SIGNS IN PRESCHOOL OR SCHOOL AGED CHILDREN
    *Difficulty following directions as compared to others
       of the same age
    Short attention span for age
    Poor language development for age
    Apt to forget what was learned
    Quickly loses interest in activities as compared to others of the
       same age; withdraws
    Difficulty in motor activities (hopping, skipping, jumping)
       as compared to others of the same age*

SIGNS IN SCHOOL AGED CHILDREN
Difficulty understanding, even after having paid attention
Inconsistent performance from one day to the next (gets a perfect paper one day and misses every item on a similar sheet the following day)
Confuses left and right
Poor handwriting
Difficulty spelling words (unfinished words, syllables omitted, words not spelled the way they sound)
Loses place when reading because of difficulty in moving eyes smoothly from left to right
Mixes up the order of words in a sentence when reading aloud or speaking
Reverses letters or entire words (mirror writing)
Poor in sports
Difficulty in copying from a book or blackboard
Difficulty learning phonics
Doesn't complete assignments or homework

6. If your child shows a number of these signs, contact your local school system - even if your child is of preschool age. The school can arrange for battery of tests and a professional diagnosis, which includes the *specific* nature of the learning disability. (Don't just settle for the label *learning disabled*.)

7. Consistently follow the advise of the experts helping your child.

OTHER COMMENTS OR SUGGESTIONS:

FAMILY ACTION PLAN: (List suggestion numbers of particular relevance and specific actions planned.)

Copyright ©1999 by Barbara Kuczen. Published by ACTIVE PARENTING PUBLISHERS www.activeparenting.com

Lying

Pass-Along-Paper 27

Description of the problem: Every child tells a lie at some time or another. Nonetheless, parents are usually quite upset when they discover a child is lying, and with good reason. When a child lies, it is often a test to see if she or he can get away with it or to learn the consequences of lying. Parents' handling of the situation is extremely important in the formation of the child's emerging value system.

Factors influencing the problem: Children tell lies for a variety of reasons. When a young child lies, it is rarely to deceive others. Instead the child is involved in fantasizing or exaggerating personal achievements. In some cases what might appear to be a lie is actually wishful thinking, a mistake in judgment, or confusion of fact with reality. The following joke illustrates this point. A small boy rushed into the kitchen and told his Dad, "I just saw a big dinosaur in the yard!" Dad scolded the child saying: "Now, Frankie, you know you didn't see a dinosaur. It must have been a big dog. I want you to go to your room and ask God to forgive you for telling a lie." The child returned a short time later, and Dad asked, "Well, did you pray to God for forgiveness?" "Yes," said Frankie, "but God said not to worry. He thought it was a dinosaur when he first saw it, too." As the child matures, lies may be a stress reaction, used when the child fears punishment or an effort to appear "good" and please parents. In some cases adults even force the child into lying. For example, when children are angry and temporarily filled with bad feelings, we force them to lie when we insist they express their true feelings. They know that saying, "I can't stand you, Mom!" will certainly result in punishment. Or, parents might unconsciously invite a lie. If your child has been warned to brush his or her teeth twice a day and you ask: "Did you brush your teeth? If you didn't, no cake for snack!" how do you think any child might respond to that question? Parents often provide children with a model that includes frequent lying. While the parent might say it is just teasing, or "little white lies," or even good manners, the child is usually not able to make these fine value distinctions. A lie is a lie, whether you say you didn't break the vase when you did or whether you tell a friend she looks lovely and later exclaim at how awful she looked. Studies show that lying usually hits a peak at approximately six-years-old and tapers down a bit at seven, goes back up slightly at eight, and then continues a steady decrease through the teen years, as children learn more effective ways of coping.

Suggestions:
1. Set a model of truthfulness. Explain why truthfulness is important, for example, being able to trust your child in the future, avoiding putting someone in danger, or preventing a problem from getting worse. Let your child know that one lies usually leads to another.
2. Make it clear that you disapprove of lying.
3. Clearly define the punishment or consequences of misbehavior. Don't make the punishment so harsh that lying is preferable to facing the consequences.
4. Demonstrate that if your child does something wrong and lies about it, the consequences will be much more severe than if the truth were told.
5. Don't try to trap your child in a lie. Give the child an opportunity to tell the truth and discuss the matter.
6. Don't invite a lie with facial expression, body language, or phrasing of a question. For example, "Cathy, you did wash your hands before coming to the table, didn't you?"
7. Help your child develop coping techniques that can be used as an alternative to lying (for example, admitting a wrong and asking how it can be corrected.)
8. Remember that the better your child's self-image, the less likely he or she is to tell a lie, since lying brings down your own concept of yourself.

9. Discipline your child in ways that don't attack self-image, or the child might feel compelled to lie in self defense.

10. Express your approval when your child tells the truth, even it if follows a lie. You might say, "I am proud of you for telling the truth. I know how difficult it was to do."

11. After your child has told a lie, discuss better ways in which your child could have handled the problem rather than lie.

12. Help your child understand that in order to prevent greater problems, the sooner the truth is told, the better. For example, if your child forgot to feed the cat, it is better to admit it than have the cat go hungry.

13. Don't encourage friends and siblings to inform on one another when someone is lying.

14. Deal with your child's lying in private.

15. Provide your child with support and assistance when the child is in a bind so that the child doesn't feel he or she has to lie to get out of a bad situation.

16. Don't argue with your child about whether or not the child is telling the truth. If you are not absolutely certain that the child is lying, it is better not to blame him or her.

17. Remember that every child make mistakes. If you punish the child or frequently react with anger, you may be promoting lying. Sometimes it is appropriate to overlook minor misbehavior.

OTHER COMMENTS OR SUGGESTIONS:

FAMILY ACTION PLAN: (List suggestion numbers of particular relevance and specific actions planned)

Copyright ©1999 by Barbara Kuczen. Published by Active Parenting Publishers www.activeparenting.com

Medical visits

Pass-Along-Paper 28

✎*Description of the problem:* A visit to the doctor can be a frightening experience for a child. Anticipating the embarrassment of undressing in front of strangers, and then being gagged by a tongue depressor, poked in the ears and nose with a lighted gadget, and finally stuck by a needle is understandably stress-producing.

✎*Factors influencing the problem:* Some children show their nervousness by becoming unusually fidgety during the long reception room wait. The annoyed parent, who can't figure out why a professional office always tells you to arrive at 2:00 p.m. when in fact they mean 3:00 p.m. is in no mood to cope with the child's restlessness. By the time parent and child enter the examining room, stress has taken its toll. The parent is so uptight that half the questions meant to be asked are forgotten. The child is experiencing fear, which can intensity the actual discomforts. Children learn their fear of the doctor. Most medical experiences contain some measure of unpleasantness. Usually one of two negative situations exists: Either the child is sick and receives an injection, or the child is well and receives an injection. However, there are some measures you can take to keep medical stress to a minimum.

✎*Suggestions:*

1. Don't tell your child there will be no shot when you know there will. Even if you think there is no injection scheduled, you are better off to say, "I don't think so, but we'll have to wait and see." Inoculations have a way of creeping up on you, and you may not think it is time for immunization when actually it is.
2. Don't ever allow your child to be injected when the child is asleep or distracted. The child should not to shocked.
3. Don't reassure the child later by saying: "That mean doctor! I didn't know he or she was going to hurt you!"
4. Don't scold, slap, ridicule, or later punish a child who was restless, crying, or fighting at the doctor's office.
5. Plan to arrive at the waiting room with toys, books, games, and other items to occupy your child's time.
6. Don't threaten to call the doctor if your child won't do something - like take medicine. Physicians should be portrayed as good, helping individuals, rather than enforcers and bad guys.
7. Don't react to your child's injection or to bad news with a look of terror, repulsion, or sadness.
8. When trying to talk to the doctor, don't outshout your child. It will only generate stress and cause the child to cry louder to be heard.
9. Don't tell your child something won't hurt when it will. Injections, certain treatments, and surgery are often painful.
10. Reassure, calm, or even hold your child during injections or treatment.
11. Explain the reasons for immunizations, physical examinations, or treatments. However, be careful about using words that are automatic stressors, such as *blood, cut,* or *stitch.* Even the words *blood pressure* can frighten a child.
12. Try to provide your own form of "lollipop" after it is all over. Your child should associate the visits to a doctor with something pleasant afterward. A stop for ice cream sundaes or the purchase of a small gift can go a long way toward minimizing the negative feelings that contribute to the stress of medical visits.

13. Don't become upset if your child exaggerates or minimizes symptoms. If it is obvious to you, the doctor will spot it as well.

14. Don't introduce your child to the doctor in a suspicious manner - for example: "Billy, this is Dr. West. She won't hurt you. She is a nice lady." Children naturally assume people they meet are nice and won't hurt them. Your mention of these words places the child on guard.

15. Tell the child what to expect if you know that one of those inoculation guns will be used. Although the device is effective, efficient, and safe, its very appearance can strike terror even in older children.

16. Let your child know the importance of a regular check-up, even when there is nothing apparently wrong. It is important to you and your child to have the opportunity to discuss growth, development, and health habits - when the child is not suffering from illness.

17. If your child must be hospitalized, arrange for a pre-hospitalization visit. Most hospitals take children on a tour of the hospital rooms, operating rooms, and recovery area. A visit can help your child feel more in control by knowing what to expect.

OTHER COMMENTS OR SUGGESTIONS:

FAMILY ACTION PLAN: (List suggestion numbers of particular relevance and specific actions planned)

Copyright ©1999 by Barbara Kuczen. Published by

Negativism

Pass-Along-Paper 29

✏️ *Description of the problem:* The negative child is often basically antagonistic and prompts a defensive or hostile reaction in others. The child may be moody, crabby, a whiner *(See Pass-Along-Paper 52)* or a pouter. The negative child is prone to perceive others as picking on him or her; often blows minor problems, setbacks, or inconveniences out of proportion; and complains bitterly or withdraws entirely from the situation.

✏️ *Factors influencing the problem:* Negative children are difficult to raise. Many parents wonder what they did wrong to create such an unpleasant child. However, some experts believe that negativism is a personality trait that children inherit right along with hair and eye color. The parent hasn't done anything wrong, and the child can't help it. Nonetheless, it is important to help your child understand his or her tendency to respond negatively to the world. While negativism may be an inborn component of personality, it is possible to identify it as a problem and learn to control it. When a negative child finds himself or herself responding negatively, the child can think, "Should I really be feeling this way, or is it just that negative part of my personality cropping up again." It is up to the parent to help the child learn to manage this difficult trait. Otherwise, the child will have problems making friends and interacting with others inside and outside of the family.

✏️ *Suggestions:*
1. Encourage your child to discuss his or her feelings.
2. Help the child get a better handle on reality (for example, asking whether everyone is *really* out to get him or her).
3. Assist your child in understanding negativism as a personality trait and coping with it.
4. Reassure the child that everyone receives occasional slights or unfair treatment.
5. Provide opportunities for success and the growth of a favorable self-image.
6. Reinforce and extend areas of behavior in which the child tends to excel and have a more positive attitude.
7. Avoid situations in which the child gains attention for negativism. (Sometimes the child uses this approach as a surefire attention getter, since attention for a negative reason is better than no attention at all.)

8. Avoid situations in which the child is placed under stress. In some cases negativism is an ineffective coping technique, used to protect the self-image by attacking the credibility or correctness of the stressor. In other words, the world's all wrong, but I'm all right.

9. Let the child take his or her time. Negative children are sometimes responding to a feeling of being constantly pressured.

10. Use positive forms of discipline, rather than punishment.

11. Structure situations in which the child experiences satisfaction from cooperating.

12. Allow the child to be herself or himself rather than threatening the self image by insisting the child act more positively - like someone else does.

13. Gently point out to the child those situations in which negativism is a form of "sour grapes." For example, the child doesn't make the hockey team and then maintains she or he really didn't want to be on it anyway.

OTHER COMMENTS OR SUGGESTIONS:

FAMILY ACTION PLAN: (List suggestion numbers of particular relevance and specific actions planned)

Copyright ©1999 by BARBARA KUCZEN. Published by Active Parenting Publishers
www.activeparenting.com

Overindulgence — Pass-Along-Paper 30

✎ *Description of the problem:* Children come into the world wanting very little. Beyond their basic physical needs, they crave security, the companionship of other human beings, recognition, and most importantly, love. During the first few years of life parents and the media teach them to want a great many other things, which might include gym shoes that cost in excess of one hundred dollars or a six hundred dollar dirt bike. Many parents question the speed with which today's children are experiencing life, acquiring possessions, and growing up. They worry that the fast pace of childhood is leaving many children jaded, bored, and spent by adolescence. For want of a better term, overindulged children are often referred to as "spoiled." These children have no concept of money. Toys, clothing, or shoes are frequently disposed of that have barely been used. It may take the child months to get around to playing with holiday or birthday gifts. After experiencing a loss, the overindulged child's first reaction is often, "Oh, well, we'll just get another." Does your child pay little attention to acquisitions once they are in the house or appear bored with a vacation or outing he or she planned? Is the child constantly searching for something else to want? Does the child always seem to find something to buy in any kind of store? If you answered "yes," your child may be confused about short-term and long-term goals and basically discontented.

✎ *Factors influencing the problem:* In many households, work substantially cuts into the time parents have to spend with children. Some parents try to compensate for their inability or unwillingness to provide enough personal attention to their children by buying them expensive gifts. Spending money on children can never be a substitute for spending time with them. Conversely, some parents have been brought up believing in self-denial and self-sacrifice so the family can have more. They dutifully deprive themselves to fulfill their children's every want and avoid infringing on the carefree days of childhood by demanding little and waiting on their offspring. In either case, the children ultimately come to believe that they are entitled to whatever their heart's desire. They equate gifts and lavish expenditures of money as a sign of love, they develop a need for acquisition, in order to feel worthwhile. Fulfillment does not come from self-actualization, but rather from satisfying selfish whims. However the sense of fulfillment is momentary, since it is the act of acquisition that is rewarding - not the thing that is being acquired. For example, Jason begs his father for an expensive pair of gym shoes, although his old pair is in good condition. Jason's father works late every evening for an entire week, but on Saturday he takes the boy to purchase the shoes he has so desperately wanted. Dad is surprised when Jason begins asking for a new component for his sound system before they are even home from the shoe store. Neither Jason nor his father realizes that the child is dependent on gifts as a tangible proof of love. It is not the thing that is important, but the father's willingness to provide it.

✎ *Suggestions:*
1. Remember that as an adult, your child's fondest childhood memories won't be of the things you purchased, but rather the special times you shared - like having a picnic or watching a sunset.
2. Guard against the "if one is good, two are better," philosophy. For example, your child asks for one package of baseball cards, but you insist on buying two, or even three.
3. Don't give in to your child's demands when you know they are unreasonable, simply because you are too tired to fight. For example, you purchase an item at the grocery check-out counter rather than dealing with your child making a scene.
4. Resist the urge to give your "squeaky wheel child" more that other children in the family who don't make a fuss.

5. Don't give in against your better judgment to your child's arguments of "Everybody's doing it," or "Everyone has one."

6. Try not to intercede when your spouse is disciplining your child because you can't stand to see the child suffer.

7. Don't allow your child to boss you around or wait on the child, reasoning that you really don't mind doing things for him or her.

8. Don't compete with other adults in the child's life to appear the most generous.

9. Don't accept just any old any excuse when it comes to letting the child off without doing assigned chores.

10. Resist your inclination to rush experiences or toys, providing them before the child is really mature enough to understand or appreciate them.

11. Don't go along with the kiddie version of keeping up with the Joneses by buying articles that are currently fashionable, even though you sense they are foolish.

12. Be concerned if your child seems to have no concept of money and thinks that the family supply is limitless.

13. Don't permit your child to keep you in emotional bondage by appealing to your sense of guilt at working, getting a divorce, or going to school.

14. Try not to create wants by calling your child's attention to the latest in toys or fashion.

15. Don't confuse your child by acting like you think it's cute when the child makes demands that reflect sophistication far beyond his or her years - for example, telling you he can't possibly play fourth grade basketball without a pair of Air Jordan gym shoes.

16. If your child enjoys going to McDonald's to eat, don't reason that a more expensive hamburger pub would be better yet.

17. If you give your child money to make a purchase, don't act unconcerned and absentminded about getting change or counting it.

OTHER COMMENTS OR SUGGESTIONS:

FAMILY ACTION PLAN: (List suggestion numbers of particular relevance and specific actions planned)

Copyright ©1999 by BARBARA KUCZEN. Published by

Poor Loser

Pass-Along-Paper 31

✏️ *Description of the problem:* The child reacts with disappointment, frustration, or anger after the loss of a game or an argument. The child wants to be first in line, first to take a turn, or first served.

✏️ *Factors influencing the problem:* Parents, as well as society, often place a high premium on competition and winning. Adults may provide a poor loser model with bad reactions to a favorite professional sports team's loss or to their child's Little League defeat. Many children's most admired role models are winning sports heroes. In addition, parents who run stress-interference for their children may be discouraging them from participating in activities where failure is likely. As a result, their children don't learn to cope with the inevitable stress of failure. Gifted perfectionists are also likely to experience this problem, since many of them are clever enough to avoid potentially unsuccessful activities. In addition, parents who are overly critical and demanding may communicate a "winning is everything" attitude. Also, when children have low self-esteem or basic feelings of inadequacy, they can be overly sensitive to a loss - which further demeans the image of self. Finally, children who are over-indulged, or "spoiled," may develop unrealistic expectations of what they are entitled to.

✏️ *Suggestions:*

1. Keep your child's age in mind. It is normal for young children to react badly to a loss.
2. Make sure competitive activities are appropriate for your child's age and developmental level.
3. Try to teach your child how to cope with losing by encouraging her or him to participate not only in activities where winning is likely, but also in activities where losing is possible. When you suspect a loss is probable, be available to provide support and reassurance.
4. Help your child apply the *rule of reason* after a loss. One loss doesn't mean you're a failure and, therefore, shouldn't devastate the self-image.
5. After a loss, help your child focus perspective. No one can be a winner in everything. Even world class athlete, Michael Jordan, didn't make it in baseball. Help your child realistically assess and appreciate areas of strength.
6. Be careful about teaching your child that *winners never quit* and instead help direct energy more productively (example - Michael Jordan left baseball to return to basketball, his strong area.)

7. If your child has a tendency to act like a poor loser, discuss better ways to behave, like congratulating the winner or saying things like, "Nice game. You really played well!"

8. Show your child that you value cooperation and having fun with friends more than winning the game.

9. Be certain that your child completely understands the rules before a game. Some children react badly to a loss because they were playing by different rules.

10. Let your child know that you value self-improvement over past performance more than beating someone else.

11. Make sure your child's coach shares your philosophy about winning and losing.

12. Teach your child some specific techniques for managing anger and frustration - such as taking a deep breath and counting to three or saying the alphabet.

OTHER COMMENTS OR SUGGESTIONS:

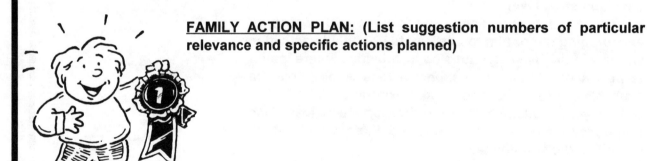

FAMILY ACTION PLAN: (List suggestion numbers of particular relevance and specific actions planned)

Copyright ©1999 by Barbara Kuczen. Published by

Problem-solving   Pass-Along-Paper 32

✎ *Description of the problem:* Solving childhood problems is the proving ground for learning how to handle challenges later in life. Children learn valuable skills in the process of working through their everyday problems.

✎ *Factors influencing the problem:* Most people have never learned a systematic method for solving problems. They attempt the process in a haphazard fashion, with no organized plan. Research has shown that certain steps are effective in problem solving. Children should be taught these steps and guided in using them to resolve problems.

✎ *Suggestions:*

Step One - Recognize the Facts:
Child and parent should painstakingly analyze what has happened to produce this problem. In some cases merely compiling the facts points to an obvious solution. For example, the child who is unhappy because her classroom teacher did not select her artwork for display in the art fair may not be disturbed if she learns that another teacher, whose opinion she does not value as highly, made the selections.

Step Two - Recognize the Problem:
After the facts have been gathered, it is important for the child to express verbally the sometimes vague sense of the problem.

Step Three - Develop a Plan:
After the problem is clearly stated, the child can work out a plan for reducing, eliminating, or controlling the situation. The plan might involve preventing future stress by withdrawing from the troublesome situation, such as the Little League team. It might involve making a conscious effort to accept the situation. Usually the formulation of a concrete plan is the first step in solving the problem.

Step Four - Suggest Alternative Approaches:
Once the primary plan has been formulated several alternative approaches must be outlined. Failure to have a backup plan will result in additional problems should the original plan prove ineffective.

Step Five - Discuss Progress at Regular Intervals:
Your child will need a sounding board to help evaluate the progress being made in solving the problem.

Step Six - Evaluate the Original Plans:
After a reasonable length of time, parent and child should confirm that the original plan (or alternative plan, if adopted) is on the right track and if it is not, the process must begin again. Perhaps the plan's failure was the result of erroneous facts, poor definition of the problem, or haphazard attempts at implementation.

OTHER COMMENTS OR SUGGESTIONS:

FAMILY ACTION PLAN: (Help your child select a problem and systematically work through the steps with the child)

FACTS:

PROBLEM:

PLAN:

ALTERNATIVES:

SCHEDULE FOR EVALUATING PROGRESS:

Copyright ©1999 by Barbara Kuczen. Published by ACTIVE PARENTING PUBLISHERS
www.activeparenting.com

Responsibility

Pass-Along-Paper 33

✎ *Description of the problem:* Caring for yourself and helping others should begin as soon as a child becomes mobile. In the process the child develops a variety of mental and physical skills, and as each new task is accomplished, the child feels competent and confident. Most importantly, the child begins to realize that he or she is not just a taker - but also a contributor - to the family. The child can assume responsibility for personal grooming, homework and studying, keeping his or her room clean, picking up toys and clothing, caring for a pet, assisting with meal preparation and clean-up, caring for a younger sibling, or working in the garden. The child may resist assuming responsibilities and frequently ask, "Do I have to?" Sometimes the child means well, but has a problem with procrastination.

✎ *Factors influencing the problem:* Ask any parents about their goals in child raising and the word *responsible* is bound to crop up amid the adjectives *happy* and *healthy.* The big question is how to foster responsibility? Booker T. Washington had the right answer. He said, "Few things help an individual more than to place responsibility upon him, and to let him know that you trust him." It is true that children develop responsibility by being responsible. However, they must get a sense of fulfillment if the lesson is to be meaningful. If a child fails to meet a responsibility or views it as a menial chore—rather then a challenge—self-esteem declines. Therefore, it is crucial that responsibilities be tailored to the competence of the child. It is impossible to force your child to be more responsible. Responsibility comes from within the child and involves a sense of duty and accountability. Responsibility develops as the direct result of performing successfully in demanding situations, rather than from parents demanding that the child act responsibly.

✎ *Suggestions:*

1. Begin early to allow your child to make choices. The child can select food, clothing, or a toy to take to Grandpa's.
2. Don't ask your child to make a choice if your mind is already made up. If you don't accept the child's choice, you end up making the child feel less responsible.
3. Don't present your child with a choice that is overwhelming. Help the child narrow the field of confusing alternatives.
4. Don't place your child in a position in which you think there is a likelihood the child will make a disappointing or frustrating choice. The child will feel irresponsible and less prone to accept his or her own judgment the next time.
5. Involve your child in plans to assign responsibilities, and provide some choice. Don't give your child all the dirty work.
6. Make a chart and schedule. Your child will probably plan to accomplish more than is reasonable and will need your guidance in establishing a more realistic program.
7. Use the chart as a means to remind your child, and avoid nagging and prodding.
8. Don't give your child responsibilities beyond his or her level.
9. Select activities that can be quickly accomplished.
10. Plan for variety.
11. Rotate the tedious, dull jobs among family members.
12. Allow enough time for your child to complete a task. Granted, dinner may be delayed while you wait for the child to finish peeling the potatoes or setting the table. However, the long-term benefits justify the inconvenience.
13. If your child expresses an interest in assuming a certain responsibility, accept the help graciously, rather than saying, "Well okay, I guess I'll let you try it."

14. Don't breathe down the child's neck. After providing a clear set of instructions or expectations, leave the child alone unless your assistance is requested.
15. Judge your child's performance according to the child's level, rather than by a fixed standard.
16. Don't compare children.
17. Follow up. Provide praise, reward, or thanks. If the child did not fulfill the responsibility, find out why. Discuss the matter. Perhaps the responsibility was unrealistic.
18. If you decide to discipline your child for failure to meet *a* responsibility, involve the child *in advance* in establishing a fair disciplinary measure so the child knows what to expect.
19. Program some flexibility into meeting responsibilities.
20. Be a responsible model for your child. If the child sees you littering, thoughtlessly messing up store displays, or trying to pull a fast one on a store clerk, expect the child to follow in your footsteps.
21. Don't underestimate your child's capability. In doing so, you are demeaning his or her self-image.
22. Help your child understand that procrastination is a means for avoiding a threatening or unappealing task. While it is effective in temporarily avoiding the unpleasant, the short-term gain is far outweighed by the stress generated.
23. Ask yourself if your child is procrastinating because he or she believes the task is too difficult or that the chances for success are minimal. Is there a lack of self confidence or competence?
24. Does your child begin an activity, but procrastinate as soon as he or she hits a snag? If so, be available to provide support and assistance.
25. Is your child procrastinating because the activity is genuinely repelling?
26. Don't be surprised if younger children lie and say they have fulfilled a responsibility when they haven't.
27. Don't ask your child why he or she hasn't fulfilled a responsibility if you know the reason is simply procrastination. Asking "Why?" only encourages the child to make up excuses. Don't accept excuses.
28. Don't lecture the child about responsibility and procrastination. It only promotes guilt and tells the child you think he or she is not capable. Instead, the child should be guided in examining the cause and ultimate outcome of the behavior. Procrastination is often a bad habit which can be corrected once the child realizes it creates more problems than it solves.
29. Help the child remember responsibilities by having him or her repeat an important set of directions. You might also encourage the child to make written notes; to place important papers in a predetermined, fixed spot; or to set aside a few times during each day when the mental question, "Now what do I have to remember?" is answered.
30. Have a bulletin board or blackboard, calendar, and note pad available in the child's room and encourage him or her to make a daily list of responsibilities.

OTHER COMMENTS OR SUGGESTIONS:

FAMILY ACTION PLAN: (List suggestion numbers of particular relevance and specific actions planned)

Copyright ©1999 by Barbara Kuczen. Published by

Risk-taking   Pass-Along-Paper 34

✏️ *Description of the problem:* Research has shown that a willingness to take risks is linked to success in later life. Childhood is a time to learn how to adjust to change and take small risks. Risk-taking allows the child to gradually grow braver, strengthen self esteem, and build feelings of personal competence and independence. Since change is inevitable and the exciting, new challenges in life are never without risk, it is important that parents encourage children to adapt to change and engage in risk-taking activities.

✏️ *Factors influencing the problem:* Some children fear change and avoid risk-taking due to basic insecurity. This insecurity may be the result of a child's basic temperament. From birth, some children seem more timid, fearful, high strung, or sensitive than others. Past traumatic experiences can also leave a child with residual feelings of helplessness. When children are experiencing illness or fatigue, they will also be less capable of adjusting to change or taking risks. They may also be psychologically weakened by a death, divorce, move, etc. Some parents contribute to the problem by exerting excessive control or being over demanding. Finally, if a child learns that the appearance of insecurity or timidity results in adult attention, the behavior is likely to continue.

✏️ *Suggestions:*

1. Keep in mind your child's age and abilities when expecting the child to take a risk or make a change.
2. Prepare your child for the new activity by discussing it and planning in advance.
3. Help your child become sensitive to change by noticing the changing seasons, growth process, or improvements in the home or community.
4. Discuss how change can create a new interest, opportunity, or improvement.
5. Analyze the ways in which humans and animals prepare for life changes, such as a change in season or birth of babies.
6. Suggest different methods for coping with the same change. Highlight the fact that there isn't just one "right" technique.
7. Evaluate the desirability of various approaches for coping with change. Consider the freedom each individual has in selecting how to deal with change.
8. Discuss whether or not change is always for the better. Recount changes in the past that did not result in improvement. Ask the child if people sometimes make a change because they think any change is good.
9. Help your child understand the strength to be gained from good basic learning skills. If you know where to go for information and can teach yourself, you can cope with the rapid changes in society.

10. Don't immediately step in to facilitate or smooth the transition resulting from change affecting your child. Give the child an opportunity to experience success in coping.
11. Encourage your child to talk about the changes affecting her or his life.
12. Make changes or take on challenges as a family.
13. Reinforce your child's risk-taking behavior by making encouraging statements.
14. Don't force your child to make changes or take risks.
15. Don't make fun of your child for being unwilling to take risks.
16. Get your child to talk about fears.

17. If possible, arrange to accompany your child to a new risky activity. Gradually try to reduce your presence.
18. If your child refuses to take a risk, like jumping off the diving board, suggest a slightly less threatening option, such as jumping off the side of the pool.
19. Try to arrange for your child to engage in new or risky activities with a friend.
20. Don't teach your fears to your child. Model a positive attitude toward risk-taking and change.
21. Let your child know that a lack of confidence and negative thinking can lead to a negative outcome. Help your child slowly build self-confidence by mastering one small challenge after another, such as climbing the jungle gym, riding a two-wheeler, or performing on stage.
22. Remember that you are trying to encourage risk-taking behavior - NOT daredevil stunts.

OTHER COMMENTS OR SUGGESTIONS:

FAMILY ACTION PLAN: (List suggestion numbers of particular relevance and specific actions planned)

Copyright ©1999 by BARBARA KUCZEN. Published by

Low Self-Esteem   Pass-Along-Paper 35

✏️ *Description of the problem:* Children use different types of information to form their self-image. Through their relationships with other people, particularly parents, they make judgments regarding their own importance. They also assess their level of competence by noting successes and failures. Children learn whether they are "good" or "bad" by comparing their behavior to the standards set by their teachers, parents, or church, and by seeing how much power they have in influencing their own lives and the lives of others. In addition, adults often tell children what they think of them. Many times children get a distorted image of themselves. They misinterpret a reaction or assign it more importance than is justified. For example, if a child is often referred to as a "little devil," the child may incorporate that perception into an unfavorable self-image. It is important to recognize when your child is suffering from low self-esteem and then to analyze the cause. Children with feelings of low self-worth may think that they have disappointed people and feel ashamed. They may not like their looks, size, or sex and wish they could completely change themselves. They might think that when they try something new, it usually goes wrong or see themselves as "quitters." Sometimes they don't handle failure well. Occasionally they sense that they could do better in school. They may feel inferior to their peers and like to play with the younger children. Children with low self-esteem may often feel nervous, afraid, or confused and dislike trying a new or strange activity. Children with a poor self-image may not like many people or feel that most people don't like them. As a result, they spend a great deal of time watching television alone. These children may wish that people would pay more attention to them and make up stories to impress others. Frequently, they need lots of praise and encouragement to keep going.

✏️ *Factors influencing the problem:* Self-image is a composite of impressions the child receives from family, teachers, friends, and others. The first component to emerge is usually the physical image. The child learns about the different parts of the body and develops a sex identity. Sometimes a particular physical characteristic gets blown out of proportion, as when the child is given a nickname such as Fat Fred or Shorty. Constant taunting provides unfavorable input and can negatively affect the second component of self-image, the psychological image, which includes the feelings and emotions concerning oneself. A second source of stress associated with self-image is the inconsistent impressions a child receives. Adults who react unpredictably to a child play a large part in contributing to the child's doubts about himself/herself. The youngster is confused when a dirty face brings warm smiles and an "Isn't she cute" one day but prompts parents to disapprove and call the child a "little animal" the next.

Suggestions:

1. Provide an environment that is steady, reliable, predictable, and responsive to the needs of the child.
2. Encourage the child to make decisions, express opinions, and practice independence.
3. Spend more time encouraging good behavior and less time punishing bad behavior.
4. Provide a clear-cut model of values and ethics.
5. Support the child when the child fails, letting the child know that there is much to be learned from failure, and that it is an unavoidable, normal part of life.

6. State your expectations, rules, regulations, and disciplinary measures in a positive way.
7. Allow time for unstructured play and exploration.
8. Be sure your child has opportunities to play with other children of the same age level and of differing age levels—both younger and older.
9. Demand that children treat adults and other children with good manners, courtesy, and kindness. Serve as a model for this type of behavior.
10. Listen when the child talks to you.
11. Encourage the child's curiosity and structure opportunities for the child to find answers through firsthand experiences.
12. Help the child develop a sense of competence with good basic reading, writing, arithmetic, and survival skills.
13. Prove that adults can be trusted.
14. Let the child know that you value compassion, caring, sharing, generosity, and helping.
15. Don't embarrass or correct the child in front of others.
16. Don't act as if the child's concerns, fears, or worries are silly.
17. Don't forget to apologize if you make a mistake, are rude, or feel crabby.
18. Don't overprotect or fail to allow the child to realize the natural consequence of a behavior. Sometimes discipline truly does hurt the parent more than the child.
19. Don't compare the child to others.
20. Let the child have some personal space in the house where he or she can store belongings and escape for some privacy.
21. Don't allow the child to downgrade himself or herself.
22. Plan a time each day to interact one-to-one with the child.
23. Don't make unrealistic demands or expect perfection.
24. Don't live vicariously through your child. When you find yourself becoming unreasonably demanding, ask yourself, "Am I doing this for the child or for myself or to please others?"
25. Show the child you value his or her input in planning a vacation or social outing.
26. Give the child some important family responsibilities.
27. Don't link self-image entirely to appearance, performance, or achievement, while overlooking the importance of kindness, sincerity, and perseverance.
28. Show the child you accept his or her individuality by providing warmth and physical signs of your love. Offer liberal, genuine praise.

OTHER COMMENTS OR SUGGESTIONS:

FAMILY ACTION PLAN: (List suggestion numbers of particular relevance and specific actions planned)

Copyright ©1999 by Barbara Kuczen. Published by

Sexual behavior

Pass-Along-Paper 36

✏️ *Description of the problem:* Certain sexual behavior is normal at various stages of development. Although troublesome to adults, this behavior causes no harm if handled properly. The most common forms of sexual behavior are touching the genitals for pleasure (masturbation) and sex play. During infancy, babies discover that manipulating the genitals can feel good. Between the ages of one and six, it is not unusual for children to rub their private parts. Masturbation becomes common again during adolescence. Sex play is a form of exploration stemming from children's basic curiosity. They want to see and touch what is hidden under clothing. Games such as "playing doctor" are common in young children. Pre-adolescents may experiment with various forms of sexual language, gestures, peeping, exhibitionism, and heterosexual and homosexual acts.

✏️ *Factors influencing the problem:* Children participate in sexual behavior for several reasons. The most basic is curiosity, but peer pressure, media influence, and the thrill of being "naughty" are also causes. Children who have been the victim of sexual abuse may also engage in self-stimulation or explicit sex play. Despite the fact that many parents recognize masturbation as perfectly normal, it is often excluded from the family sex education program. Parents will discuss reproduction, birth control, and sexually transmitted diseases, but omit any mention of masturbation. While children are interested in all aspects of sex, masturbation is the subject that is most timely and relevant. It is the one component of their sexuality that is here and now. Minimally parents should teach children that masturbation is a private act. Meanwhile, unless masturbating becomes a continuous activity through which the child is trying to find relief or distraction from other stresses, don't let it become a source of undue concern. Some experts think that it is a form of sex education, in which children learn about the body.

✏️ *Suggestions:*

1. Reduce your child's sexual curiosity by frankly discussing issues at an age-appropriate level. There is no need to over-explain or give more information than the child requests or needs.
2. Monitor your child's exposure to sexually explicit programming in the media.
3. Supervise your child's play. Plan interesting activities so that sex play does not result from boredom.
4. Set rules and explain that certain behavior (sex play) may seem like fun, but that it is inappropriate. Let visitors to your home know the rules.
5. Don't make your child feel guilty about masturbation or sex play. The disapproval or disgust that parents associate with a child's early sexual behavior can cause confusion. The child begins to think that sex is dirty and pleasurable feelings are wrong.
6. You make want to consult your pediatrician to be certain that rubbing the genitals is not a sign of vaginal or bladder infection that is causing pain in these areas.

7. Many experts believe that by the time a child is eight, parents should have begun to teach about how women and men have intercourse, the dangers of AIDS and other sexually transmitted diseases, homosexuality, abortion, and birth control.

8. Remember that discussion of sex should also include teaching about morality and responsibility.

9. Role play and practice with your child ways of saying "NO!" to unwanted sex play or sexual advances.

10. Point out to your child that other parents won't want you to play with their children or visit their homes if you engage in masturbation or sex play.

OTHER COMMENTS OR SUGGESTIONS:

 **FAMILY ACTION PLAN:** (List suggestion numbers of particular relevance and specific actions planned)

Copyright ©1999 by Barbara Kuczen. Published by

Shyness

Pass-Along-Paper 37

✏️ *Description of the problem:* Most children experience a temporary fear of strangers at approximately six months of age, and throughout childhood sporadic stretches of shyness are normal. Physical changes, stress, or factors connected with the stage of development can contribute to it, but children soon return to their old selves. However, if the condition persists, it can limit a child's social life, cause the child to be overlooked, or inhibit creativity. People often underestimate the intelligence of a shy child.

✏️ *Factors influencing the problem:* Studies show that many shy children grow into shy adults. They are anxious in social settings and introverted. In some relationships they may seek constant attention, which usually grates on the nerves of the adults they continuously "bug." The shy-passive child seeks reassurance, acceptance, and approval. Instead of speaking up when angry or insulted, he or she may instead resort to indirect expressions, such as dawdling or simply not doing as told. The problem can result from a lack of security, poor self-image, or overprotection. Children who have suffered chronic illnesses can develop the trait. In some cases shyness is a reaction to stress. The child does not know how to cope or has been punished, criticized, and ridiculed so often that he or she simply withdraws from social situations. In a few cases shyness is the result of a lack of practice in meeting and interacting with others. Sometimes, the shy child has similarly shy parents. Some experts believe that we attach too much importance to competition which whittles away at the self image of the child who does not tend, by nature, to be competitive. The child who suffers from a poor self-image and lack of confidence, rather than facing failure, withdraws. Acknowledge your child's individuality. Children differ in the way they approach life. If your child is not outgoing, it doesn't signal a fault. Accept the child as is, rather than pressuring him or her to be more friendly or talkative. Trying to force your child to make personality changes can create a problem. You are in effect telling the child there is something wrong with the way he or she is. This knowledge will only cause the child to be more shy and fearful of his or her ability to cope with social situations.

✏️ *Suggestions:*

1. Keep punishment and criticism to an absolute minimum.
2. Use some of the suggestions in *Pass-Along-Papers 24 and 35* for building a sense of independence and a strong self-image.
3. Avoid situations in which the shy child is directly interacting with a particularly aggressive child, who may either totally ignore or harass the shy child.
4. Enroll the child in courses or recreational programs where success can be experienced, such as an arts and crafts class, team sport, or choral group. Be careful of placing demands on the child to perform solo or to get into the limelight.
5. Ask the teacher to seat your child next to another quiet or shy child.
6. Ask the teacher to provide opportunities for your child to be noticed by the class without experiencing a lot of pressure: for example, passing papers, delivering notes, or holding the door.
7. Encourage and reinforce social interaction. Let the child give a party.
8. Help the child develop alternative means for coping with stress. Use some of the stress-management techniques suggested in *Pass-Along-Paper 42*.
9. Discourage the child from downgrading himself or herself.
10. Tell the child not to call himself or herself shy and try to change that mental image. Explain that some people are more quiet by nature.
11. Point out the child's many strengths and help him or her to improve in areas of need.

12. Praise your child when he or she initiates interaction with others but do not force this interaction.
13. Teach your child the basics of making conversation. Rehearse possible conversation starters, such as "What is your favorite television program?" or "Have you taken any trips lately?"
14. Teach your child the basic social conventions, such as shaking hands, opening the door for others, or answering basic questions, such as "How are you?" Model this behavior for the child.
15. Prepare your child for new social situations, by discussing them at home first. Let the child know what to expect.
16. If possible, prepare your child for a new situation, such as attending a new school, by visiting before the first day.
17. Try to arrange for your child to participate in a new activity with a friend with whom she or he is comfortable, for example taking ballet lessons or playing on the soccer team.
18. Encourage your child to play with younger children, who will probably make him or her feel less shy.
19. If possible accompany your child to new social situations to provide support and comfort.
20. Do not contribute to your child's shyness by letting the child off the hook when she or he complains of not wanting to participate or being afraid.
21. If possible, do not force the child to stay alone in situations in which he or she does not feel comfortable.
22. Do not ridicule the child for being shy or allow friends or siblings to make fun.
23. Take into account your child's developmental level when deciding upon reasonable expectations in new social settings.

OTHER COMMENTS OR SUGGESTIONS:

FAMILY ACTION PLAN: (list suggestion numbers of particular relevance and specific actions planned.)

Copyright ©1999 by Barbara Kuczen. Published by

Sibling rivalry   Pass-Along-Paper 38

Description of the problem: Siblings are jealous or hostile toward one another. The rivalry can be expressed in competitive behavior. Older children, in particular, tend to express their rivalry more competitively - while younger children push, grab, hit, and tease. Sibling rivalry stems from the threat that a brother or sister will become more important and loved by the parents. It is common for young children to experience strong feelings of sibling rivalry when a new baby enters the family. A child may actively show hostility; revert to baby talk, bed wetting and soiling pants; or act out resentment on the parents.

Factors influencing the problem: Quarreling among siblings is perfectly normal. Living in close proximity is bound to create certain stresses, and the family provides a tolerant environment in which individuals can spontaneously express themselves, without fear of looking bad or being rejected. Minor squabbling among siblings can teach children how to cope with competition and rivalry outside the home. Sibling rivalry is the proving ground for learning how to solve problems and respect the privacy and belongings of others. It can also teach children how to stand up for themselves, express their feelings, and resolve conflicts. However, when sibling rivalry becomes excessive it can result in bitter feelings that last a lifetime. Siblings sometimes behave aggressively and destructively against one another and develop long term feelings of antagonism and indifference.

Suggestions:

1. Consider your children's developmental level. Quarreling among family members is normal at any age, and two year olds, for example, are bound to bicker, push, hit, and grab.
2. Be certain that you are not contributing to the problem by showing favoritism to one child over another.
3. Realize that if one sibling has a special talent or is obviously superior to the other in academic or athletic ability, jealousy is likely to occur - particulary if the two children are of the same sex. Make a special effort to show that you value the less talented child.
4. Spend equal amounts of time building the special interests of all children in the family. Don't spend a lion's share of your time and money on the one child who is obviously more gifted. Spend equal amounts of money on clothing for each child. Younger children shouldn't have to wear nothing but hand-me-downs.
5. Do not compare your children. Point out each child's unique and special characteristics and traits.
6. Avoid babying one child more than another, especially if they are close in age.
7. Avoid having a pet nickname for one child only.
8. Spend time alone each day with each of your children.
9. Provide children with their own special belongings and private place. Insist everyone in the household respect the rights of ownership and privacy.
10. When you shop for holiday gifts or vacation souvenirs, buy each child something different - based on their unique interests.
11. Resist the urge to buy all the children the same *cute* outfits for a special family event.

12. In order to prevent squabbling over chores, set up a weekly schedule of family responsibilities so that everyone knows what must be done and who will do it. Equally divide the "dirty work."

13. Have family meetings to make important decisions and air complaints. Let the children participate in determining the consequences if rules are broken.

14. Set up time limits for each child to talk on the telephone or use the computer. Work out a system for deciding who will select television programs for viewing.

15. Arrange for siblings to spend time away from each other, pursuing their own interests with their own friends.

16. Don't insist that older siblings take their younger siblings out with them.

17. Don't rely too heavily on older siblings to babysit younger children.

18. Don't allow older children to tease or to constantly correct or discipline younger children. Tell older siblings that discipline is your job.

19. Don't over-protect younger siblings, which only creates friction with the older children.

20. Prepare a young child for the birth of a sibling well in advance. Allow the older child to help care for the new baby. When gifts are purchased, there should be something for each child in the family - not just the new baby. Explain to the older child that a new baby means extra work and less time, but that you still love the child very much. Expect your child to revert to babyish behavior and express resentment. Don't punish the child, but instead offer reassurance of your love.

21. Arrange to spend time together having fun as a family. Remember that sibling rivalry can result from a child's over-reliance on the parents for love and attention. Plan for the entire family to meet these needs for one another.

22. Try as much as possible to ignore the squabbles between siblings. Realize that it is almost impossible to be an impartial referee unless you have witnessed the incident.

23. Encourage your children to express their feelings and anger openly and honestly.

24. Set firm limits for what will and will not be tolerated, for example - no hitting, no name-calling, no picking on a sibling's known areas of vulnerability.

25. Remember that taking sides only encourages more sibling rivalry. Help all your children realize that siblings are no threat to parental love.

OTHER COMMENTS OR SUGGESTIONS:

FAMILY ACTION PLAN: (List suggestion numbers of particular relevance and specific actions planned)

Copyright ©1999 by Barbara Kuczen. Published by

Speech problems   Pass-Along-Paper 39

✏️ *Description of the problem:* The child stutters, uses baby talk inappropriately or is hesitant to talk, particularly when away from home.

✏️ *Factors influencing the problem:*

Stuttering: When a child stutters, the child tries to say a word, hesitates, and then repeats the word again. It may be the first letter or the whole word which is repeated. Stuttering is normal in children between the ages of two and four years old. It usually lasts for just a few months. Between the ages of six and eight years of age, children may begin to stutter again, with the problem lasting for several years. The most serious form of stuttering begins between the ages of three and eight years old and continues unless some therapy is used. Stuttering after five years old is considered a more serious problem than stuttering in the preschool years. Approximately 2% of school aged children stutter, with boy stutters outnumbering girls four to one.

Baby talk: Most children who deliberately use baby talk do so for attention. Adults may laugh, listen, or tell the child, "Don't talk like a baby." Children may also revert to baby talk after the birth of a sibling, in an attempt to recapture the position of only child and baby in the family. Also, sometimes older children will baby talk as a means to go back to a time when life was easier.

Hesitant speaking: A child who is able, but unwilling to speak, may do so for a variety of reasons. First, the child may not need language - as adults respond to body language, grunts, or even anticipate needs. A child may also be reluctant to speak because of shyness *(See Pass-Along-Paper 37.)* A shy disposition results in a failure to speak unless the child is in a secure and comfortable environment. A dominant adult, teacher, or peer can also intimidate a child into not talking. Sometimes a child with limited English, a limited vocabulary or minor speech impediments will also be hesitant to talk in public.

✏️ *Suggestions:*

1. Determine the exact nature of your child's speech problem. Voice disorders, lack of fluency, and poor articulation deserve prompt attention. So do any other physical or emotional factors identified with your child's speech problem. Consult an expert who may recommend hearing, speech, and developmental testing.
2. Don't allow other children to tease or mimic the child.
3. Allow the child to finish speaking. Don't become impatient, interrupt, or finish the sentence for her or him.
4. Don't constantly correct the child's speech. Nagging will ultimately cause the child to just keep quiet.
5. Don't attempt to work on all speech errors at once. Take things one at a time.
6. Don't assume that the child can correct speech problems simply by putting a mind to it. Stuttering or poor speech habits require great effort for improvement.
7. Build the child's self image by structuring opportunities for success.
8. Try to prevent the child from feeling guilty about the problem. No one is to blame.
9. Encourage the child to practice speech by engaging in daily conversations.
10. Provide your child with a good speech model.

11. Try to prevent the child from becoming self-conscious about speech. Don't discuss the child's problem or progress with other adults while in the child's presence.

12. If the child stutters, don't ask the child to stop, take a deep breath, and start over. This practice is annoying and only adds to feelings of inadequacy.

13. If the child is hesitant to speak and asks for things by pointing or grunting, tell the child, "I don't know what you want. You will have to tell me." Don't anticipate in advance that the child wants juice, or a television channel change, etc. and act accordingly. If you do, there is no need for the child to use language to express wants and needs.

14. If your child seeks attention, but doesn't talk, don't respond. For example, the child may stand a short distance away and begin to fidget or act restless and whimper. Don't go to her or him and ask, "What's the matter?" or run down a laundry list of possible needs. Instead wait for the child to approach and speak first.

15. Try to engage the child in conversations by asking questions and modeling language. If the child refuses to talk, walk away. Don't give the child more attention for not talking than for talking.

16. If the child uses baby talk, first consider the child's developmental level. Is it deliberate baby talk or the child's level of emerging language.

17. Don't reinforce your child's baby talking by giving the child undue attention. If the child asks to be held or hugged in baby talk, say, "I'd love to hold you, but you must use good language to ask me."

18. If the child talks to you in baby talk say, "I can't understand you when you talk that way," and turn away. When the child begins to speak appropriately, immediately give the child your attention.

19. Consistently follow the suggestions of speech therapists who are helping you to solve your child's speech problem.

OTHER COMMENTS OR SUGGESTIONS:

FAMILY ACTION PLAN: (List suggestion numbers of particular relevance and specific actions planned)

Copyright ©1999 by Barbara Kuczen. Published by

Stealing

Pass-Along-Paper 40

✏️ *Description of the problem:* The child knowingly and without the permission of the owner takes something that doesn't belong to him or her. Minor stealing is common in young children particularly between the ages of five and eight. If your child continues to steal past the age of ten, consider it a serious problem.

✏️ *Factors influencing the problem:* Preschool children are in the process of understanding the somewhat difficult concept of ownership. The young child is also still trying to learn impulse control, so when he or she desires something, the most natural response is to just take it. Although this behavior is normal, adults must help the child develop morals and ethics, as well as impulse control. As the meaning of ownership and a conscience develop, stealing usually stops. While it is important to help your preschooler understand that stealing is not socially acceptable, you should not make the very young child feel guilty. Older children may steal as the result of stress, peer pressure, or an intense desire for an object - without the money to buy it. Sometimes a child has a low self-esteem and attempts to feel "big" or "tough" by stealing. Also, if you don't have self-respect, you probably won't respect the rights or belongings of others. Still other children may simply enjoy the excitement of stealing. As the child approaches ten years old, if stealing is still a problem consider seeking professional help.

✏️ *Suggestions:*

1. Begin early in life to explain the concepts of ownership and borrowing.
2. Don't provide a poor model. For example, don't take small objects from hotels or restaurants or change price tags at the store.
3. Closely monitor your child and be alert for new toys, clothing, or other belongings which you didn't buy.
4. If you suspect your child has stolen something, immediately discuss the matter.
5. If your child admits stealing, arrange to give back what was taken.
6. Confront your child's stealing privately.
7. Don't use cute words such as *sticky fingers* or *borrowing* to soften up the discussion of what the child has done. Refer to the theft as *stealing*.
8. Don't preach to the child about stealing, but instead ask the child how he or she would feel if they lost something by theft.
9. Model appropriate behavior by asking to borrow items from your child. Return them promptly and in good condition.
10. Insist that your child return items borrowed in a timely fashion. Objects lost or damaged should be replaced by the child.
11. Make your child aware of the consequences of stealing, for example - embarrassment, losing friends, getting suspended from school, or even going to jail.
12. Let your child know that even if others take your objects, that is no excuse for taking things from them.
13. Help your child figure out ways to earn money for things desired.
14. Don't tempt your child to steal by leaving money laying around or your purse or wallet wide open.
15. If someone tells you that your child has stolen something, you will be shocked and likely to deny it. Keep an open mind and get all the facts.
16. Try to determine the causes for your child's theft. Solve the underlying problems.

17. Don't accept any excuses for stealing.

18. If your child steals once or twice every two weeks, regularly check the bedroom and pockets for unfamiliar objects or large amounts of money. Research shows that the fear of being discovered is a deterrent. Stealing can quickly become a habit, especially if it is easy to get away with it.

19. Don't dismiss your child's stealing as unimportant, a phase, or a problem that will soon be outgrown. Take direct action to stop it.

OTHER COMMENTS OR SUGGESTIONS:

FAMILY ACTION PLAN: (List suggestion numbers of particular relevance and specific actions planned)

Copyright ©1999 by Barbara Kuczen. Published by

Step-families   Pass-Along-Paper 41

✎ *Description of the problem:* In response to the accelerating divorce rate, step-families are increasing in number. Remarriage results in step-parent/step-child relationships that generate a set of very unique and complicated issues. Some experts believe that the older the child, the greater the adjustment difficulty, but it is dangerous to generalize. In dealing with your specific situation, you might find that your three year old cannot cope, while your twelve year old eases into the new relationship. The problems experienced by a child affected by remarriage are complex, in that they cannot be totally separated from the anxiety produced by the original divorce. The child has helplessly watched as his or her other world was shattered and may be fearful of it happening again or leery of making a commitment to a step-parent that might end in heartbreak. Sometimes a child blames the step-parent for contributing to the divorce - even irrationally, as when the step-parent and parent weren't even acquainted at the time. This tendency might be precipitated because the child has been clinging to the idea that parents would ultimately reunite. Remarriage completely obliterates this last shred of hope. If the child has made a satisfactory adjustment to the divorce, chances are the single-parent arrangement is quite comfortable and intimate. There may be jealousy or fear that this special bond will become weakened.

✎ *Factors influencing the problem:* It is important to deal with any of the problems mentioned above before the remarriage, because once the new family structure is in place, everyone involved is bound to experience some difficulties. You can help ease the transition by waiting a reasonable length of time before considering remarriage and informing your child of the decision well in advance. Remarriage should not be considered during the child's painful "mourning" period. It is also wise to plan for a gradual get-acquainted period, in which the possibility of marriage is discussed. When the announcement is made, it is important to warn the child to expect everyone to have some adjustment problems, rather than painting a rosy picture of living happily ever after. However, research findings indicate that children raised in step-families do not differ significantly from their counterparts reared under the traditional family structure. Once the initial adjustment is over, they share the same problems, behaviors, successes, and failures.

✎ *Suggestions:*
1. Allow your child to vent hostile reactions and express fears and concerns.
2. Your child should realize that the new relationship will take time, and that he or she will be involved in making it work. Most children can accept the challenge, since a warm, secure family situation is equally important to them.
3. Once you're settled as a new family, don't be inclined to attribute every problem to the step-family arrangement. All parent/child relationship go through some sticky times.
4. You can expect the new relationships between child and step-parent, child and step-brothers or step-sisters, and step-parent and ex-spouse to result in some friction and accommodating adjustments. You may even find that you and your new spouse differ on some of your ideas regarding the functioning of your new family. Differences in values, backgrounds, lifestyles, and disciplinary techniques will require a certain amount of give-and-take. Young children may experience confusion over such minor matters as the term used for going to the bathroom or the manner in which a holiday is celebrated.
5. Emphasize the idea of being a family, rather than delineating all the various step-relationships. Don't insist that a child call your new spouse "mother" or "dad" against her or his will.
6. Be honest with yourself about your emotions. You may even be feeling guilty because you sense you don't particularly like your step-child, although you love the mother or father of that child.

7. Acknowledge the fact that if you have natural children in one household and step-children in another, balancing your attention, love, and money can be a difficult task.
8. As a step-parent, expect resentment from the ex-spouse, step-children, and even your spouse.
9. Don't come on like gangbusters, immediately asserting your authority. Live with the existing rules and regulations until the child has settled into the new relationship.
10. Recognize when your step- child is testing your love. Uncharacteristic misbehavior may be calculated to find out just how deep your feelings run.
11. Don't compete with the natural parent, and don't allow the child to make comparisons. Tell the child nothing can ever change the special bond between natural parent and child. However, you hope to develop another type of special relationship.
12. If the child informs you that you are not doing something like the "real" mother or father, thank the child for the information but explain that every individual is different.
13. Don't take sides in disputes between your step-child and the ex-spouse or between your spouse and her or his ex-spouse.
14. Realize that initially the child may be looking for a carbon copy of the absent parent and expect you to fit the mold.
15. If the absent parent was neglectful, the child may resent you for being too good, in order to defend the parent's image. The image of the natural parent is often linked to the child's self image.
16. Don't leave discipline matters solely to the natural parents. Slowly become involved and assert yourself -explaining to the child that you are responsible for his or her well being too.
17. Expect the angry child to challenge your authority by retorting "You're not my real mother (or father)!" You might respond by saying, "You are absolutely right, but that doesn't change the fact that I love you very much and that I am concerned about you."
18. Don't be surprised if the child is embarrassed because his or her mother now has a different last name.
19. Understandably, a child who is not faced with the added stress of moving, adjusting to a new school, and finding new friends often adapts more easily.
20. Don't expect step-children and step-parent to experience love at first sight, but by working together to solve the problems, they can grow to love one another.

OTHER COMMENTS OR SUGGESTIONS:

FAMILY ACTION PLAN: (List suggestion numbers of particular relevance and specific actions planned)

Copyright ©1999 by BARBARA KUCZEN. Published by

Stress-breakers   Pass-Along-Paper 42

Description of the problem: Once the child has identified that the stress reaction is present by tuning into the physical and behavioral warning signs *(See Pass-Along-Paper 44,)* it is time to use techniques that work to get out of the fight or flight response and regain equilibrium.

Factors influencing the problem: Stress reactions can occur fifty or more times a day. Therefore, it is important that everyone know some techniques for getting out of these frequent fight or flight reactions, which can ultimately create physical or emotional wear and tear. There are hundreds of techniques, several of which are presented in the *Suggestions*. The idea is to introduce your child to a smorgasbord of equilibrium-regaining techniques from which to select what works best for him or her. Not every child will use every technique presented. The idea is to introduce a wide variety so that the child might find one or two that feel comfortable.

Suggestions:

1. Your young child can be taught a simple rhyme to help control stress generated energy, stop angry outbursts and promote conflict resolution:
>Take a deep breath and count to three,
>Say please stop and listen to me!

2. An older child will benefit from using an easy, effective breathing technique developed by Elizabeth and Charles Stroebel for the Mesa, Arizona school system. It is called Kiddie Q.R. (Quieting Reflex) and works as an instant neutralizer for the shallow breathing that ushers in the fight or flight response. Controlling breathing can help head off the other side effects of stress. The quieting reflex is easy to learn and takes only six to ten seconds:

   Step One: Recognize the physical signs of stress, especially the shallow breathing.
   Step Two: Deliberately relax your facial muscles, then consciously form a smile in which the corners of your mouth point upward toward your eyes. Concentrate on feeling calm.
   Step Three: Take a long, deep breath. Four slow counts in and four slow counts out. Repeat a second time, but not more than three times.
   Step Four: As you exhale slowly, open your mouth and let your jaw droop. Imagine feelings of heaviness and warmth traveling downward from your limp jaw to your toes.

3. Teach your child to put on a happy face. Researchers have found that a smiling face creates normal heart rate and skin temperature. Imitating a frightened face, on the other hand, leads to a racing heart, cold hands, and perspiration - even when you're not really frightened. Experts speculate that their findings may explain why smiles are infectious or how anger can turn a crowd into a mob.

4. Next time your child is feeling stressed, nervous, and tense, encourage him or her to physically project the image of one who is relaxed and efficient. Unclench the hands, drop the shoulders, and concentrate on letting go of muscle tension. Consciously breathe deeply and speak more slowly. If possible find some open space to take a two-minute mini-walk and deliberately stride in a controlled, unhassled manner, gently swinging the arms.

5. Adults and children regularly need time out. It is a time to get away from it all, think, and regroup. Time out should be a privilege extended everyone in your home. If used properly it will not be thought of as a punishment. You may find that occasionally you suggest your child take a time out in order to avoid disruption or confrontation. In such cases it is best not to order the child into the bedroom or time-out area for a designated time period, but instead explain, "I realize that

you are upset, but I cannot allow you to upset the entire household. Please take a time out until you are feeling better. If you want to talk, call me." The child is free to rejoin the family when he or she feels ready. If the time-out concept is used effectively, you will find that your child asks you for cool-out privileges. You may even want to have some DO NOT DISTURB signs available for adults and children to use when they need some privacy.

6. Try adding music to the time-out area. Also, pets make excellent visitors in the time-out room. We know that stroking a pet can relieve stress and actually reduce blood pressure. Heart rate also improves when people gaze at fish swimming in a tank, fire burning in the fireplace, surf, a Lava Light, or a mobile.

7. Aroma therapy is a relatively new area, but the basic concept is hardly revolutionary. We all know how soothing the smell of certain fragrances or foods are. Like a picture, one scent can be worth a thousand words and can recall pleasant feelings and images from the past. If the whole family is tense, baking bread or cookies can act like a tranquilizer.

8. A massage is an excellent way to help your child ease muscle tension, improve circulation, and stimulate the entire nervous system. It also lets your child know that you care and are there for him or her.

9. Many tapes are available to guide relaxation, some designed specifically for children. In addition to using tapes, you can also teach your child to pretend to be a movie producer. Tell the child to design a very peaceful, relaxing set. It might be a forest scene, a beautiful seashore, or a relaxing stream side. The child imagines being in the middle of the set as the movie is played on the back of the eyelids or inside of the forehead. Tell your child not to think of any other thoughts and to refocus on the image should attention wander.

10. One of the body changes caused by stress is muscle tension. You can help your child to recognize when stress is present by identifying the signs of muscle tension before things get out of hand, and to learn how to release this tension through relaxation. Many of the following steps are adapted from Dr. Herbert Benson's book *The Relaxation Response*.

Step One	Lie down in a comfortable position (even if the child can't lie down, once the child is proficient at controlling the release of muscle tension, it can be done when the child is seated at a desk, on the bus, or playing a game.)
Step Two	Close your eyes
Step Three	Breathe deeply through your nose.
Step Four	Beginning with your feet and working upward, first tense and then relax your muscles (feet, ankles, legs, hips, fingers, wrists, arms, back, shoulders, buttocks, neck, jaws, face, and eyes). Tense each muscle group for five seconds. Study the tension so that you will be able to identify it in the future. Now deliberately let go of the tension. Imagine it flowing out of your body like an ice cube melting in hot water or a stone making concentric circles when dropped into a lake. Your body feels warm and heavy. The relaxed muscles feel as if they are sinking into the floor or bed. It feels as if you have thick, warm oil in your veins. Concentrate on the relaxed condition for at least twenty seconds before tensing the next group.
Step Five	After you have completely relaxed all your muscles sit quietly for a few minutes.
Step six	Breathe normally for two or three minutes before getting up.

OTHER COMMENTS OR SUGGESTIONS:

FAMILY ACTION PLAN: (List suggestion numbers of particular relevance and specific actions planned)

Copyright ©1999 by Barbara Kuczen. Published by ACTIVE PARENTING PUBLISHERS
www.activeparenting.com

Stress - coping   Pass-Along-Paper 43

✏️ *Description of the problem:* The child shows signs of stress *(see Pass-Along-Paper 44.)* Another name for stress is the *fight or flight response.* It occurs when an individual experiences a situation that is perceived as threatening, thereby causing an internally triggered physical and emotional reaction. Hormones are released which prepare the person to fight or flee. Total freedom from stress is impossible, and stress is actually vital to a healthy person. However, when stress is extreme or chronic, it can cause wear and tear on physical or emotional health.

✏️ *Factors influencing the problem:* Any stimuli which is personally threatening to an individual is a stressor. The child experiences stress as a result of thoughts concerning real or imagined threats. The most common sources of stress are social and psychological. In the process of normal development, nature provides children with an opportunity to deal progressively with a variety of stressors. Each stage of development produces social and emotional changes that require the youngster to cope. For example, a two-year-old child often begins resisting parent influence in order to demonstrate independence. In addition, some stressors - such as parents' divorce, death of a loved one, personal illness, or a family move - affect children at any age. It is important for parents to view the difficult aspects of each stage of development as a learning experience for the child. As the child grows and matures, valuable coping skills are gained. Coping with childhood stress is the proving ground for handling stress in later life. Growing up has never been easy, but it has never been harder than in today's society. Modern children not only face most of the same stress their parents faced when growing up - the old standbys such as peer pressure, sibling rivalry, separation anxiety, and coping with school - they also face a host of new stressors which were virtually unheard of a generation ago. For example, young children are well aware of the violence on our streets or the dangers of AIDS. When it comes to stress, many modern children face a double whammy. On the one hand, they face more stress than in the past, dealing with the old sources of stress as well as the new. On the other hand, there has been erosion in three of the traditional forms of stress support: the family, the school, and the community.

✏️ *Suggestions:*

1. Remember that stress is not always bad. Controllable stress motivates and can increase creativity and productivity. For example, test taking is a notorious stress provoker. Stress prompts the student to study and can activate peak performance during the actual examination. Only if there is too much stress, and the student becomes overly anxious and is unable to prepare or "blanks out" and forgets the answers is there a problem.

2. Your goal is not to eliminate all the stress from your child's life. Even if you could, the result would be dull. Consider the following example: A preschooler just can't get a puzzle piece to fit. As the youngster becomes visibly stressed, some concerned adult rushes over and inserts the piece. At this point the child usually becomes troubled. The stress is over. The puzzle piece is safe in its spot. Yet, somehow, the child doesn't quite feel satisfied and can't understand why. It is much more beneficial for children themselves to learn to control stress in gradually increasing amounts than it is to have stress interference run by parents.

3. Research has proven that it is possible to learn stress management and relaxation techniques that work. However, you and your child must accept the fact that it is possible to manage stress. You must expect to succeed at the task. If you expect to fail, you certainly will. Stress management techniques must be learned *(See Pass-Along-Paper 42.)* As with any new skill it takes time to become proficient. Neither you nor your child should expect overnight results.

4. Stress management is a continuous process, to be constantly revamped in response to new stressors, new experiences, and maturity.

5. Explain the stress reaction to your child. The depth and detail of your discussion will be determined by the child's ability to understand. Children as young as three years old can comprehend the basics of stress. It is a good idea to talk about the fight or flight response, which we have inherited from our cavepeople ancestors. Children can easily give examples of times in which they felt and almost uncontrollable urge to fight or to flee from stress.

6. Next teach your child to monitor her or his body. The child can't control stress until she or he has learned to identify its presence. Tell your child that everyone is born with a stress-detector, which includes a set of early physical signs of stress which are usually quite obvious. Your child might be convinced that everyone can spot her or his sweaty palms, pounding heart, rapid breathing, or trembling. Reassure the child that actually most people can't tell when someone else is stressed. Rather than feeling self-conscious the child should assume responsibility for regaining control *(See Pass-Along-Paper 42.)*

7. Your child should also learn to recognize the behavioral changes that occur over a longer time period, such as bad dreams or withdrawal from school and social activities. A complete listing is included on Pass-Along-Paper 44. You may want to post it on the refrigerator and discuss it with your child.

8. You should help your child identify the coping strategies he or she uses when stressed. Discuss which work and which don't. Figure out alternatives for the ineffective ones.

9. Teach your child techniques for getting out of the fight or flight response and regaining equilibrium *(See Pass-Along-Paper 42.)*

10. After your child has regained equilibrium and is able to think clearly, it is time to pinpoint the source of stress in order to try to resolve the issue. Often the stressor is apparent, as would be the case if the child didn't make the basketball team. But sometimes the problem is not obvious. The way to pinpoint the stressor is to observe your child closely. See if there is a pattern to the stress signals. Next discuss your observations with your child. You may not know why the child behaved in a particular way, but you can say, "I noticed that you aren't sleeping very well," or "You used to love school, but lately it seems you hate to get up in the morning."

11. After you have pinpointed the stressor, apply problem solving techniques *(See Pass-Along-Paper 31.)* Help the child focus perspective. Many children tend to magnify the seriousness or importance of rather minor life events.

12. One of the major tasks of socializing a child is teaching him or her how to control and use stress generated energy. A toddler's temper tantrum provides an excellent example of the tremendous primitive energy that builds internally from stress. If a child doesn't learn socially acceptable means for venting, he or she may react with acts of violence, vandalism, aggression, and acting out behavior.

13. Teach your child to seek out support and help if needed. Also model ways of providing support so your child can help others in times of stress.

OTHER COMMENTS OR SUGGESTIONS:

FAMILY ACTION PLAN: (List suggestions number of particular relevance and specific actions planned)

Copyright ©1999 by Barbara Kuczen. Published by

Stress signals   Pass-Along-Paper 44

✏️ *Description of the problem:* Children under stress send off signals. Parents should pay attention to sudden changes in a child's behavior, particularly when the changes exist in more than one area. For example, a child who wets the bed one night is not necessarily a child who is under stress. However, if the child was formerly dry and suddenly begins to wet the bed frequently, has night terrors, and reverts to dependent, babyish behavior, the child may, indeed by stressed.

✏️ *Factors influencing the problem:* Fortunately in younger children the behavioral signs of stress are often quite obvious. Bed-wetting, night terrors, and dependency are hard to miss. However, as children mature, the behavioral signs of stress are not always as easy to identify. It might take some time for a parent to notice than an older child is developing eating disorders, withdrawing from school and social activities, or retreating into a fantasy world of computer games. Therefore, the older the child, the more important it is for that child to be able to recognize indicators in his or her own behavior. The checklist that follows can help you and your child identify the physical and behavioral signs of stress. It includes four categories: *Physical Reactions, Fight Reactions, Flight Reactions,* and *Spillover Reactions.* If you do see signs of stress in your child, check out *Pass-Along-Papers 42* and *43.*

WARNING SIGNS OF STRESS
Physical Reactions

- Acne, rash, or other skin problem
- Belching attacks
- Bruxing (teeth-grinding)
- Change in appearance
- Chest pains
- Cold, clammy hands
- Dizziness
- Faintness
- Frequent urination
- Headaches
- Hiccough attacks
- Increased number of illnesses
- Increased number of asthma attacks
- Increased pulse rate
- Indigestion, diarrhea, stomach upset, queasiness, vomiting, or undereating
- Menstrual irregularities or cessation
- Muscle spasms, pain or tightness in jaw, neck, shoulders, or back
- Nervous tics or twitches
- Pale, wan look
- Pounding heart
- Shortness of breath, hyperventilation, or overbreathing
- Tearing eyes
- Wide-eyes look caused by dilated pupils

Fight Reactions

- Acts of violence or vandalism
- Aggression or hostility
- Boasts of superiority
- Criminal activity
- Daredevil stunts
- Firestarting
- Testing or defying authority
- Use of bad language
- Unusual difficulty getting along with friends
- Impatience
- Negativism
- Rudeness or brattiness
- Self-harm or self-abuse
- Stealing
- Tantrums
- Unusual jealousy of close friends or siblings
- Vicious acts against animals or other people

Flight Reactions

Clinging dependency
Dislike of school
Downgrading of self
Escapism - preoccupation with:
   Television or movies
   Video or computer games
   Imaginary friend
   Superheroes, such as Superman
   Rock stars or other celebrities
   Animals, including dinosaurs
   Sports heroes or sports teams
   Horoscopes, astrology, good luck charms, or occult interests
Excessive daydreaming
Excessive sleeping
Infantile or regressive behavior
Listlessness of lack of enthusiasm
Loss of interest in activities usually approached with vigor
Lying
Overeating
Procrastination, making excuses
Quiet, solitary behavior
Rigid conformity to rules and regulations
Scapegoating
Sexual behavior
Shyness
Smoking
Thumb-sucking
Uncontrollable urge to run and hide
Use of alcohol
Use of drugs
Withdrawal from school or social activities

Spillover Reactions

Bad dreams
Bed-wetting or soiling pants
Biting or picking at fingernails
Changing tone of voice
Clearing throat frequently
Compulsive cleanliness
Decline in school achievement
Demand for constant perfection
Easily startled
Frequent explosive crying
General irritability
Increased number of accidents
Insomnia
Nervous laughter
Nervous mannerisms or hand movements
Night terrors
Poor or fitful sleep
Restlessness, shifting in seat, hyperactivity
Stuttering or stammering
Talking faster
Tense body, such as hands making fists or shoulders hunched forward
Uncharacteristic carelessness
Uncharacteristic poor concentration

OTHER COMMENTS OR SUGGESTIONS:

FAMILY ACTION PLAN:

Copyright ©1999 by Barbara Kuczen. Published by Active Parenting Publishers www.activeparenting.com

Talking Back   Pass-Along-Paper 45

✎ *Description of the problem:* The child makes disrespectful or rude comments or gestures to adults. The child challenges the adult's authority and has to have the last word.

✎ *Factors influencing the problem:* Children model their behavior based upon their observations of others. If your child sees other children talking back, the child will probably try it. Also, if your  child sees you talking to others in a rude fashion or using impolite hand gestures while driving, the child may model your behavior. Children learn what they live, and if you speak to your child and to others respectfully your child will probably do likewise. Realize that it is normal for children to get *sassy* around the *terrible twos.* They will sometimes aggressively challenge adult authority again during the adolescent years. (*See Pass-Along-Paper 12 - Defiant Behavior*) Try to identify when your child is most likely to talk back. Is it when he or she is tired, frustrated, or feeling overworked? Does the child talk back to one person more than any other, for example - a grandparent or teacher? Identifying a pattern can help you figure out how to solve the problem.

✎ *Suggestions:*

1. Don't humiliate or talk down to your child. Speak the way you want her or him to talk to you and to others.
2. Don't discipline or embarrass your child in front of others. Wait until you can privately discuss the problem. Children will sometimes talk back in front of their friends in order to save face.
3. If your child talks back to you in front of your friends, remind the child that you try not to create embarrassing situations in front of his or her friends and that you expect the same courtesy in return.
4. Remember that children frequently talk back for attention. If your child talks back in public, immediately remove the child to a private location.
5. Tell your child that if he or she wants to question your authority it should be done privately, not at a family party, shopping center, or restaurant.
6. Calmly discuss issues about which you and your child disagree, but don't get into a heated argument, which only promotes talking back.
7. Teach your child the appropriate way to question authority or to disagree. Tell the child it is important to clearly state your opinion, listen politely to the other person's position, calmly make comments or raise new issues, and accept the final decision. Model this approach in your disagreements with other adults.
8. Don't allow your child to talk back one day and discipline the child for the same behavior the next day. Be consistent in your approach to talking back.
9. Don't contribute to the problem by making impossible demands on your child.
10. Make certain that your child understands what is expected and when it must be completed. Don't encourage talking back by arguing with your child once you are certain that the child understands your expectations. If the child protests, say, "You know what you have to do," and walk away.
11. When you give your child directions, warn the child ahead of time that you will only say it once.
12. Clearly define the consequences in advance for talking back and enforce them consistently.
13. If you hear your child talking back to a relative, teacher, babysitter, or other adult, immediately remove the child from the situation. Let the child know exactly what he or she said that was wrong.
14. Enlist the help of relatives, teachers, and babysitters in discouraging your child from talking back.

15. Don't talk to your child in a confrontational manner which encourages the child to talk back. For example, instead of saying, "Get in there and do your homework right now!" try saying, "I know you have a lot of homework tonight. Don't you think it's time to start doing it?"

16. Don't surprise your child with sudden demands which may provoke anger or frustration which leads to talking back. Let the child know far in advance what is expected and when. Have a consistent list of responsibilities and encourage the development of time management skills by having your child plan in advance when these obligations will be met.

OTHER COMMENTS OR SUGGESTIONS:

FAMILY ACTION PLAN: (List suggestion numbers of particular relevance and specific actions planned)

Copyright ©1999 by Barbara Kuczen. Published by Active Parenting Publishers www.activeparenting.com

Tantrums   Pass-Along-Paper 46

✎ *Description of the problem:* When frustrated, angry, or upset the child reacts with a variety of behaviors, including throwing himself or herself on the floor, crying, screaming, kicking, head banging or pounding fists. Tantrums are most common in nonverbal preschoolers who are unable to cope and cannot express their feelings. However, older children, and even adults, may respond to frustration with physical acts of violence, shouting, or swearing. Nearly every child will try a tantrum at some point, sometimes after seeing it work for another child. Your reaction will determine if this form of behavior persists.

✎ *Factors influencing the problem:* Some children have a lower frustration level than others, which can make them more likely to have angry outbursts. However, the most significant factor is how the parent handles that first temper tantrum. Children learn coping strategies through trial and error, and many remain with them into adulthood. When children find that fits of rage result in satisfaction, they are apt to rely on tantrums in times of stress. Let's say you give in to your child's tantrum at the grocery store because you know that the child is sick or tired. You buy that candy or toy he or she demands. Maybe you are just so embarrassed you want to settle your child down as quickly as possible. Well, expect the child to have another tantrum the next time he or she wants a treat while shopping. You have taught your child that throwing tantrums will ultimately satisfy his or her wants, or at least gain the child a lot of attention. Tantrums are effective, logical coping strategies. Your biggest concern in dealing with them is to prevent their recurrence.

✎ *Suggestions:*
1. Are you raising your child in a restrictive environment, controlled by many "don't's" and "mustn'ts?" If so you are probably contributing to her or his frustration. Allow your child to be independent and do things for himself or herself.
2. Are you inconsistent, forbidding a behavior on one occasion and tolerating it on the next?
3. Determine the situations that typically stimulate a tantrum. If you recognize that your child has a temperament that includes a low frustration level, perhaps you can avoid some of the outbreaks by removing the frustration or intervening when the child is overtired.
4. If you sense that your child is about to erupt, go to the child and try to help solve the problem, such as assisting with a frustrating task or preventing another child from taking a toy away.
5. Tell your child you know how he or she feels and encourage him or her to express the feelings in words.
6. Ask the child what can be done to correct the situation. If the child is unable to think of any solutions, suggest some.
7. Help your child carry out the solutions.

8. Praise the child for handling the difficult situation in an appropriate way.
9. In the event a tantrum does occur, don't try to stop it or console the child. Your child's behavior may terrify you, but children rarely hurt themselves. In fact, tantrums usually subside when there is no audience.
10. If you are afraid to leave your child alone during an outburst for fear of injury, remain in the same room but pay no attention. Even glancing at the child can intensify or sustain the tantrum. Also, be careful not to express your concern with your body language.
11. Don't respond to the tantrum by losing your temper and engaging in explosive behavior.
12. If your child has a tantrum, don't lose your composure, particularly if you are in a public place or in the presence of friends or relatives.

13. Don't allow a tantrum to work by meeting your child's demands.
14. Don't allow a tantrum to work by reducing your demands on the child.
15. Don't try to reason or talk sense to the child when she or he is in a rage.
16. If a sibling or playmate tells you that the child is having a tantrum, tell him or her that you know, but you can't talk to your child until the tantrum stops.
17. When the tantrum is over, approach the child with a reassuring hug - but don't discuss what just happened. If the child starts back up, immediately walk away again.
18. After the child is calm discuss the causes for the tantrum. Ask your child what he would do if you behaved similarly. Rehearse alternatives for the next time a situation arises and discuss consequences for the next time a tantrum occurs.

OTHER COMMENTS OR SUGGESTIONS:

FAMILY ACTION PLAN (List suggestion numbers of particular relevance and specific actions planned)

Copyright ©1999 by Barbara Kuczen. Published by Active Parenting Publishers www.activeparenting.com

Tattling   Pass-Along-Paper 47

✏️ *Description of the problem:* The child constantly tells adults about the little things that others do wrong. It is sometimes difficult to explain to children the difference between tattling and appropriately informing adults about serious acts of misbehavior, destruction, accidents, or emergencies.

✏️ *Factors influencing the problem:* If adults pay little attention to the tattling child and take no action based on the tattler's report, he or she will soon learn that it is pointless to tattle. On the other hand, if the child is able to get others in trouble, there is a real payoff for tattling. The tattler will continue to *snitch* in order to feel powerful, get even, or gain attention.

✏️ *Suggestions:*

1. Communicate a clear set of rules about tattling.
2. Make certain that your child understands the difference between minor acts of misbehavior which are better off ignored (such as occasionally saying a bad word), and information which should be reported (such as emergencies, injuries, fights, or destruction of property).
3. When your child tattles don't respond to the report. Act only on observed, firsthand information.
4. Don't reinforce your child's tattling by dropping everything to go check the child's report each time your child tattles.
5. Be consistent in the way you handle your child's tattling. Don't respond to the tattling one day and ignore it the next.
6. Supervise your child's play closely enough that you know what is going on and, therefore, tattling is unnecessary.
7. When you suspect that your child is coming to you to tattle, stop the child immediately and ask, "Is this something really important that you can't solve without me?"
8. If the child begins to tattle refuse to listen.
9. Teach your child how to solve problems without tattling. For example, the child might talk it out, walk away, ignore the problem, or warn the other child to stop misbehaving so that he or she doesn't have to tell.
10. Enlist the help of relatives, teachers, and babysitters in ignoring your child when he or she tattles.
11. Discuss with your child how other children feel when the child tattles.

12. Point out that other children do not like to play with a child who tells on them for every little thing.
13. Before your child has a guest or visits a friend, remind your child about when it is appropriate to tell and when telling is just tattling.
14. Praise your child for ignoring another child's minor misbehavior, rather than tattling.
15. Show your child that you value cooperation and getting along with others.

OTHER COMMENTS OR SUGGESTIONS:

FAMILY ACTION PLAN: (List suggestion numbers of particular relevance and specific actions planned)

Teasing

Pass-Along-Paper 48

✏️ *Description of the problem:* The child ridicules others or calls them unflattering names. A child who is the victim of frequent teasing can suffer a decline in self esteem. Teasing usually provokes a strong reaction. The victim may react with tears, denial, or anger. Over the long-term, he or she can become fearful of social contacts and withdraw from others. The child doing the teasing observes these responses and realizes his or her power to hurt others. In addition, adults react to the teasing by not only paying attention to the victim, but also to the offender.

✏️ *Factors influencing the problem:* Try to determine if there is a pattern to the teasing. Does your child tease others when angry, excluded from an activity, frustrated, or told "no"? Is your child more likely to tease younger children, shy children, the same child, friends of the same sex, or older children? Identifying a pattern can help you better understand your child's problem and solve it. For example, your child may put down other children in an effort to bolster his or her own self image. Although the teaser will find that adults and other children don't like name calling, the negative reactions may not be enough to outweigh the satisfaction the child gets from having the power to hurt others

✏️ *Suggestions:*

1. Try to determine the cause for your child's teasing. Does the child tease others in order to boost his or her own feelings of inadequacy? If so, try to arrange for your child to experience feelings of competence and positive self worth from appropriate behavior.
2. If the teacher complains that your child teases others at school, determine if he or she is frustrated by work that is too difficult. A child who cannot gain attention for positive achievements will often settle for negative attention over no attention at all. A poor student may try to inflate his or her image of self by putting others down.
3. Is the child bored because lessons and activities are too simple? Are there enough materials to go around? Is your child teasing others for amusement?
4. Try to pay as little attention to the teasing child as possible. Instead, turn your back to the teaser and comfort the victim.
5. While is it relatively easy for you to ignore the teasing, the child who is being teased is likely to react strongly - reinforcing the teasing behavior in the offender. Separate the two children and try to calm the upset child as quickly as possible. Distract the victim with conversation and some interesting activity. If the teased child continues to complain, express understanding and say, "Sally sometimes forgets how to talk to others."
6. Try to establish an atmosphere in your home in which everyone ignores the teasing.
7. Enlist the help of relatives, teachers, and babysitters in ignoring your child when the child teases others.
8. When your child begins acting appropriately, pay attention. Make it clear that it is the teasing you don't approve of - not the child.
9. Praise your child when you see him or her getting along with other children. Let the child know that you value the ability to cooperate.
10. Don't allow older siblings to model teasing behavior by name calling or poking fun at a younger child in the family.
11. Communicate the rules about teasing and name calling in your home.

12. After your child has behaved rudely by ridiculing, name calling, or embarrassing someone, discuss exactly what was wrong with the behavior. Discuss how the other person probably felt. Ask your child to put himself or herself in the other persons place. For example say, "How would you feel if your sister told people that you wet the bed?"

13. If poking fun is your brand of humor, realize that children have difficulty understanding the fine difference between harmless and hurtful teasing. Your child may only be following your lead.

14. Remove your child from the presence of others when the child teases.

15. After your child teases someone, discuss alternative ways to behave.

16. Before your child has guests or interacts with others, provide a reminder that rude behavior is not acceptable.

17. Supervise your child when he or she is playing with someone who is the frequent victim of the child's teasing.

18. Make certain that your child understands that when you tease others you not only hurt their feelings or make them mad. Over time, other children will avoid you.

19. Talk to your child about the differences in people and about various challenging conditions, such as blindness, difficulty learning, or needing a wheelchair.

OTHER COMMENTS OR SUGGESTIONS:

FAMILY ACTION PLAN: (List suggestion numbers of particular relevance and specific actions planned)

Copyright ©1999 by Barbara Kuczen. Published by

Television

Pass-Along-Paper 49

✎ *Description of the problem:* Many children today can hardly imagine a time in history when families read, listened to the radio, or played games in the evening. Research findings indicate that more than 62% of two-year-olds sing commercial jingles and the average twelve-year-old has seen 300,000 television commercials. Many teachers complain that television viewing is a passive experience, in which young children hear language, but do not practice using it to express themselves. These teachers also suspect that the frequent interruption of programs with commercials may condition children to have short attention spans. The average preschooler watches over 40 hours of television per week. By the time the child graduates from high school, he or she will have spent approximately 11,000 hours in classrooms, and over 15,000 hours watching television.

✎ *Factors influencing the problem:* Television can have good, as well as bad, effects on children. There are a number of programs of excellent quality which can stimulate a child's curiosity and expand knowledge, as well as entertain. The problem seems to be that some parents do not limit viewing to this type of programming, and their children spend hours watching shows that contribute nothing positive to their development. In fact, television can model violence *(See Pass-Along paper 51)*, foul language *(See Pass-Along-Paper 10),* and a casual approach to sex *(See Pass-Along-Paper 36)*. In addition, children can get a distorted image of what is attractive. When children watch television, they usually do little else. They don't move about - except to change the channel or get a snack (which can lead to the development of young couch potatoes.) They don't talk or interact with other individuals. In other words, the time spent in front of the television is not contributing to gross or fine motor development, verbal ability, or social skills. Children learn best through firsthand experiences, but everything on TV is secondhand. In addition to poor motor skills, inadequate verbal ability, and difficulty with social interaction, students may develop poor listening skills. Despite the fact that they spend hours listening to the television, the level of programming that youngsters prefer (situation comedies, cartoons, quiz shows, as well as frequent reruns) does not encourage children to listen carefully and precisely. Preschool teachers report that many children don't seem to know how to structure their own play activities. Teachers in all grades are often surprised at how late children stay up watching television on school nights. Homework often takes a backseat to viewing and ends up sloppily done or not done at all.

✎ *Suggestions:*

1. Discuss as a family the amount of time spent viewing television each week.
2. Agree to cut-back on viewing. Don't try to go *cold turkey* and stop watching television altogether. Be careful not be too rigid, or your efforts probably won't work for long. Credit yourself with making progress if you can cut-back on viewing and break your child's habit of turning on television with near-reflex-action.
3. Review the weekly schedule and mutually determine those programs most intellectually nourishing. Watch only high-quality shows, but be careful about having too long a list of *forbidden* shows, which can sometimes become that much more enticing to children.
4. Be sure you know what your child is watching and join in the viewing, if possible. Following a show, discuss new concepts or ideas with your child.
5. Talk about feelings. Did the program make viewers feel happy, sad, fearful, or angry?
6. Analyze commercials and how they try to appeal to the consumer to buy. Vow not to purchase junk.

7. Immediately turn-off any program that you feel is exceptionally violent, sexually explicit, or in poor taste.
8. Discuss whether or not the characters on television are like people in real life.
9. Discuss with pre-adolescents and adolescents the likelihood of most of us actually looking like one of the characters on *Baywatch.*
10. Plan alternatives to fill the time previously spent watching television. You might consider reading (parent to child, child to parent, or independently), taking up a new hobby, taking a walk or bike ride, playing board games, listening to recordings of old radio dramas, physical exercise, a community activity, or playing with friends.
11. Discourage television viewing when guests visit.
12. Remember that television can influence your child's values. If, as one study suggested, the average fourteen-year-old has seen 11,000 televised murders, how upset can we expect the child to become at murder 11,001?
13. Television often models violent reactions to stress and conflict.
14. Young children can usually not distinguish commercials from the programming. Commercials tell children of all ages that we need their products to cope with life. We may need a pill to feel better, a toy to have fun, a car to prove that we've "made it." As a result children learn that we must look beyond ourselves to these products to help us cope, and the well-being of the self-image becomes linked to the satisfaction of mass-produced standardized needs. The child's constant *gimme-gimmes* can be a source of tension between the parent and the child. In addition, a frustrated child who finds he or she can't make a toy do the things it did on the commercial may be angry at the parent for buying the item, rather than at the advertisement for misrepresentation. Television commercials contribute to a materialistic society and create wants and artificial needs in individuals of all ages.
15. Some preschoolers cannot separate fantasy from reality. Television can make the fantastic seem very believable and real to the young child. They are confused when they see an actor die on one show, only to reappear an hour later on another program. They can react with fearfulness, fearlessness, or confusion. Be sure to monitor your child's viewing and discuss the differences between reality and fantasy.

OTHER COMMENTS OR SUGGESTIONS:

FAMILY ACTION PLAN: (List suggestion numbers of particular relevance and specific actions planned)

Copyright ©1999 by Barbara Kuczen. Published by ACTIVE PARENTING PUBLISHERS
www.activeparenting.com

Time (quality)   Pass-Along-Paper 50

✏️ *Description of the problem:* The family has a limited amount of time available to share each week. Parents work and children are busy with school, friends, sports, and other extracurricular activities. On a typical week-day, the family may only have three hours together in the evening before the children go to bed. This time is often spent on homework, chores, or television viewing.

✏️ *Factors influencing the problem:* It has often been said that it is not the quantity of time spent with children, but rather the quality that counts. While it is possible to mesh work and parenting, it is essential to recognize the importance of making the limited time shared by parent and child count. Also, a few *high quality* minutes shared each day is not enough. No one can arbitrarily assign a minimum number of clock hours required for parenting each week. However, it is obvious that one hour shared in front of the television set each evening is not enough. Remember that all time spent with your child will not be *high quality*. No parent manages perfectly. You will occasionally lose control of your time and your temper. You will feel incompetent, inefficient, and just plain tired. Although you realize that your toddler just wants to be close, you will be annoyed at constantly tripping over the child who follows you from room to room. You may resent the invasion of your privacy when you are interrupted in the bathroom. Sometimes when you are ready to spend some *high quality time* your child will be busy and want no part of you. Experts make time management sound easier than it actually is. However, it is possible if you work at it and become better organized. The result will be more time to spend with your child. Use this time to form the bond of special memories. When your child is grown and recounts his or her fondest childhood memories, it won't be the expensive gym shoes you bought that comes to mind. It will be something you did together, like a picnic or camp-out in the yard.

✏️ *Suggestions:*

1. Take time to really look at your child. Notice signs of illness, emotional upset, weight gain or loss, poor grooming, or changes in development.
2. Spend more time listening. Ask about everything - from how things are going in school to how your child likes the lunches you are preparing.
3. When your child is facing a crisis, drop everything and offer support, understanding, and assistance in working through the problem. Let the child know that he or she is more important to you than a job or community service.
4. Share laughter. Let your child show you how to be a child again and appreciate the humor in a silly joke or funny accident.
5. Try to see the world through your child's eyes. Delight in a first snowfall or romp in the pile of leaves you just raked.
6. Take up exercise that can be shared with your child. Cycle, swim, jog, or jump rope together.
7. Make dinner a special family time. Resist the temptation to alternate between local fast food establishments each evening. Discourage eating in shifts or in front of the television set and use the time around the table for family discussion.
8. Teach your child restaurant etiquette, and when you do dine out make it a family event.
9. Make shopping trips leisurely family excursions. Share in clipping coupons, planning meals, discussing prices, and considering nutrition. Top off the day with a stop for ice cream.

10. Use automobile travel time for discussion and planning instead of listening to the radio.
11. Work side-by-side to accomplish household chores.
12. Carefully consider any children's extracurricular activities that take away from precious family time. Attempt to schedule these activities when the child would normally be at a sitter's.
13. Be selective about any community service that does not directly involve your child. Instead, try coaching a team, running a children's club, or helping at school.
14. Refuse to give up prime evening time to work overtime or stop for a drink with friends.
15. Guard against parallel parenting, in which parent and child are engaged in the same activity (such as television viewing) without actually interacting.
16. Remember the importance of starting the day right, which includes not only a good breakfast, but also a warm happy send-off. Always join your child at breakfast, even if you only have coffee.
17. Turn off television and play a game. When watching TV, discuss programming.
18. Plan family vacations. If you want some time away from the children, there are numerous resorts, ski lodges, cruises, camps, and hotels that run child care programs.
19. Find ways to involve your child in cooking, yard work, repairs, cleaning the basement, sorting through drawers, or giving a party. Suggest your child chat with you as you prepare a meal or clean up afterward.
20. Tell your child how you feel. Explain the reason for rules, punishment, and displeasure. Let your child know that nothing ever affects your love. Good kids sometimes do bad things.
21. Give your child kisses, hugs, pats on the back, and handshakes.
22. Say, "I love you," every day.

OTHER COMMENTS OR SUGGESTIONS:

FAMILY ACTION PLAN: (List suggestion numbers of particular relevance and specific actions planned.)

Copyright ©1999 by Barbara Kuczen. Published by

Violence

Pass-Along-Paper 51

✎ *Description of the problem:* The child hits, punches, bites, kicks, or throws objects in an effort to hurt another or to protect possessions. The child may also shout or destroy property when angry or frustrated.

✎ *Factors influencing the problem:* Some individuals have more difficulty controlling their tempers than others. The media provides children with a violent model for conflict resolution. Parents may inadvertently do likewise. Children model the behavior they observe in others. If you spank your child you may be teaching him or her to respond violently to stress. If you scream or slam things around when you are angry or frustrated, expect your child to follow your example. Try to determine what triggers your child's violent reactions. Does the child frequently go-off when tired, frustrated, arguing, attempting to take something away from someone else, or in self-defense? Is your child more likely to go after younger children, older children, children of the same sex, or adults? Identifying what sets off your child can help you plan how to solve the problem. Remember that violence is a natural reaction to stress. Younger children are more likely to give-in to their urge to strike-out when angry or frustrated. The young child learns that hitting, biting, kicking, and throwing objects are actions that always get noticed. So does shouting or destroying property. Until the child can use language to effectively express feelings, violent reactions are all they know how to use. As they grow, we must help children learn non-violent ways to vent their stress.

✎ *Suggestions:*

1. Avoid situations that provoke a child to respond violently, such as forcing the child to do something, overcrowded conditions, a shortage of materials to go around, or intense competition.
2. When your child behaves violently, first determine if the victim is injured. Then immediately remove your child from the presence of others. Leave the child alone and try not give him or her too much attention, which reinforces violence as an attention-getting technique.
3. If necessary, physically restrain your child from hurting others. Put your arms around the child, but don't show anger, which may only further provoke him or her.
4. Help your child understand exactly what he or she did that was wrong. Although nearly every child knows that violence can hurt others, your child may justify what happened because another child hit first, wanted to take a toy away, or said something insulting.
5. Recognize that biting is quite normal in two-year-old children, who are still at an oral phase of development. Furthermore, the two-year-old cannot empathize with the feelings of others. Your two-year-old probably doesn't quite realize what he or she did wrong and may become confused if you get too angry.
6. Biting has become a major health issue in day care centers and pre-school programs. As soon as a child can understand, you must communicate that biting is a totally unacceptable way of handling conflict.
7. Help your child learn to express anger and resolve problems by talking, rather than resorting to violence. If your child is having trouble expressing feelings, say, "What is bothering you?" If the child can't seem to verbalize feelings, you might ask a question like, "Did you throw the blocks because Johnny knocked over your tower?" If the child shakes the head, "yes," then ask the child to repeat back what you said in order to learn how to communicate about problems.

8. After the child has verbalized the problem, ask the child what can be done. If she or he comes up with a solution, offer praise for the child's good thinking. If the child can't think of any solutions, suggest some. If your child accepts one of your suggestions, have the child repeat it back to practice using communication skills to solve problems.

9. If the children involved in the incident work through their difficulties, praise their ability to problem solve and get along.

10. Teach your child some techniques for controlling angry impulses, like taking a deep breath and counting to three, counting backwards from ten, or saying the alphabet.

11. Tell your child to ask an adult to help before he or she loses control and hurts someone else.

12. When the child uses alternatives to violence in coping with stress, be sure to catch him or her being good and offer praise.

13. Keep your eye on a possibly explosive situation, and intervene before things get out of hand.

14. Teach your child to monitor personal stress levels in order to regain control before behaving violently. Teach the child some stress management techniques.

15. Help your child understand the consequences of hurting others. For example, other children won't want to play with you or parents won't allow you to visit their home.

16. Be certain that other children or older siblings are not deliberately provoking your child.

17. Inform the parents of playmates that your child sometimes loses control of his or her temper so that they can keep a better eye on things when the child is visiting.

18. Enlist the help of relatives, teachers, and babysitters in helping to curb your child's violent reactions to stress.

OTHER COMMENTS OR SUGGESTIONS:

FAMILY ACTION PLAN: (List suggestion numbers of particular relevance and specific actions planned)

Whining   Pass-Along-Paper 52

Description of the problem: Whining usually has a nasal tone, which is a variation of the child's normal voice. The child whines when he or she is tired, wants something, is unhappy about a decision, doesn't want to follow the rules, is disappointed or frustrated, or wants to complain about something. Parents often list whining as their child's most annoying behavior. Whining can become a habit and part of the child's regular method of communicating. Although whining does get attention, often it is in the form of adult irritation, exasperation, or anger. Whining can ultimately lower your child's self esteem, as he or she experiences frequent negative reactions from others.

Factors influencing the problem: Every child whines at some point or another, particularly between the ages of three and five. When speaking in a normal tone of voice doesn't result in adult attention, the child logically tries another tone. How you respond to the whining will determine how long your child continues to whine. If you give in to the child's demands because you can't stand to listen to the whining, he or she will learn that it works and continue to whine. Don't contribute to your child's whining by failing to consider the child's age and developmental level. For example, if you expect too much from your child, like accompanying you on an all-day shopping trip, she or he is likely to get tired and beg to go home. Also, ask yourself if your child is begging for something that is appropriate. If all of the other children have in-line skates, your child probably really wants a pair and needs them to participate with the group. Try to determine if there is a pattern to your child's whining. Does the child whine at a particular time of the day, in response to certain demands, or when engaged in certain activities? Is whining a request for help, a form of complaining, a bid for attention, a way of indicating injury, or an attempt to get his or her own way? If you do discover a pattern, it will be easier for you to anticipate when whining is likely to occur and make a plan for dealing with it.

Suggestions:

1. Make it clear that you will not listen to whining.
2. When your child begins to whine, say, "You are whining. I will listen to you when you stop." Then walk away, continue to do what you were doing, or talk to someone else.
3. If your child whines and wants you to do something for her or him which you know the child is capable of accomplishing alone, ignore the child's pleas for help. Walk away and say, "I know you can do it yourself."
4. Teach your child alternatives to whining, such as talking about feelings, asking for help, walking away from a frustrating situation, taking some time out, or counting backwards from ten when angry.
5. When your child is calm and happy, rehearse ways to ask for things in the future without begging or whining.
6. Be certain that your child knows the rules, the exact nature of her or his responsibilities, and what is expected in various situations. For example, if you visit the zoo, explain that there will be stuffed animals for sale in the stands and in the gift shop, but that you are not going to buy any. Once you announce your intent, don't decide to surprise your child and reverse yourself once you get there. If you do, you will be showing your child that your decisions are not final and encourage him or her to whine or beg to get you to change your mind.
7. Enlist the help of relatives, teachers, and babysitters in your efforts to stop your child's whining. Do not allow the child to go to another adult and beg for his or her way after you have said, "No!"
8. Explain the reasons behind the rules, responsibilities, and decisions you make.

9. Don't get upset when your child whines. If he or she sees you react, the whining is more likely to continue.
10. When your child whines, immediately remove her or him from the attention of others.
11. Try to get a tape recording of your child whining. Play it back when the child is calm and discuss how the whining sounds to others.
12. If your child stops whining and communicates in a normal tone of voice, offer praise and say, "Good, now I can listen to you."

OTHER COMMENTS OR SUGGESTIONS:

FAMILY ACTION PLAN: (List suggestion numbers of particular relevance and specific actions planned)

Copyright ©1999 by Barbara Kuczen. Published by

Notes...

Notes...